Pure Joy's

LIFE THROUGH THE WRONG END OF MY BINOCULARS

Joy Smith Walsh

Pure Joy's Life Through the Wrong End of My Binoculars
Joy Smith Walsh

Published April 2023
Heirloom Editions
Imprint of Jan-Carol Publishing, Inc.
All rights reserved
Copyright © 2023 Joy Smith Walsh

This book may not be reproduced in whole or part, in any manner whatsoever, without written permission, with the exception of brief quotations within book reviews or articles.

Disclaimer:
The writing style of grammatical and punctuation corrections followed the author's instruction and preference and not the writing style standards preferred by Jan-Carol Publishing, Inc.

ISBN: 978-1-954978-86-7
Library of Congress Control Number: 2023936099

You may contact the publisher:
Jan-Carol Publishing, Inc.
PO Box 701
Johnson City, TN 37605
publisher@jancarolpublishing.com
www.jancarolpublishing.com

Dedicated to . . .

My family who had to love me

Keith, who chose to love me

For my son, Brad, now loving me from heaven

INTRODUCTION

As a special gift to all, I thought of a poem or prose, but a poet laureate I am not! A beautiful song came to mind. Sadly, that talent too is lacking. I know the tribute was there. It was merely the question of, "In what form?"

Reflecting on my own childhood, it occurred to me that my gift would be a reminder of the many kindnesses and memories my family gave to me, perhaps a reminder as to how we impress children in simple ways with words and acts.

If you are looking for a style of writing following all the rules of grammar, be warned—the style is all mine!

I present to you the following pages: a personal tour through the labyrinth of my little child memory bank, intertwined with the grateful heart of the grandmother, Joy, as I weave the colorful tapestry of surprises, truthiness, stories, and miracles. In contrast, the younger members of my family simply were not around, just as there are some members that live on in our hearts and sweet memories.

This simple tapestry is woven with strong fibers, areas "designed" by members who now reside in our memory. My wish is that the younger generation will continue to "spin" and "weave," adding their personal style to a family heirloom. Speak with the "music of your heart." The weaving continues…

TABLE OF CONTENTS

Personal Stories
Those Magical Binoculars 1
The Power of the Pins 3
How Do I Write in a Whisper? 6
The Hill 8
I'm How Old? 11
Age and Time 13
A Wrinkle of Time 15
Stitched with Heartstrings 18
After the Carnage and Chaos 19
Where Did Autumn Fall? 23
A Special Person Came Knocking 26
A Wish for My Son 28
Love of a Scottie 30
May/December Love Story 33
Treat Me Like a Dog Please! 35
I Miss Having Sciuridae 38
My Life Heroes 40
Greatness for Something-or-Another 42
A Palace from Pallets 43

Family Stories

"I Wish for You" To My Grandchildren 45
Common Cents and Double Nickels 48
Where's the Love? 50
A Tisket a Tasket – My Special Basket 52
Brother, Where Art Thou? 54
Her Secret Garden 56
Daddy's Catastrophic Day 59
Blonde True Stories 61
Michelle's Little Doll 63
Matthew's Little Big Miracle 64
There's My Star 66
Eulogies of Life 68
Things That Make Ya Go HUMMMMMM 70
Our Smith-Sonian Smokehouse 72
The Seat of History 75
I Gave the Best of What I Never Had 77
He's Had His Moments 81
A Personal Christmas "Carol" 84
She is Our Sunshine 86
Heavenly Sunshine 88
Nature's Art Museum 94
Ed's Elfin Era 96
King Memorial Church 99
It's Just a Doll 101
That Simple Life 103

Humorous Stories
Family Rumblings 105
Consumers Lose 107
Southernese Shortcuts 109
It's Jest English... 112
Acts of Compassion & Humanity 115
Domino Days/Nights... 118
My Close Call with the "Garden Klatch" 121
Worn Out Words.. 124
I Want One of Dem Designer Labels 126
What if My Question Doesn't Match 129

Spiritual Stories
Just Hold My Thought 132
I Graced Her Walk... 134
God's Quilt of Life 136
Divine Humor... 138
Bleak Outlooks and Bright Lookouts 140
Shining For You 142
Luke's Song.. 143
Heavenly Escorts 145
Father, Do I Have to Go? 150
Would You Know a Broken Soul? 152

Patriotic Stories
Patriots Still Serving 154

Epilogue 159

PERSONAL STORIES

Those Magical Binoculars

I'm sure you skim through these topics I have presented, as you run across the term "looking at life through the opposite end of binoculars." I think it is important to interpret the DEPTH of that statement. Perhaps another way to say the same is "think outside the box," yet that isn't how I felt!

Haven't we all wondered about truths and meanings? Haven't we wondered what the destiny of the world we live in could or will be? Do you realize how we communicate in symbols, numbers, forms, logos, etc.? Well, I chose to symbolize through words, hoping to conjure happy memories by walking you through my life from childhood through a half century of living. What's more important is that if you focus to understand, then you will.

All aspects of life we must discover within rise to accomplish most of what we expect of ourselves—goals, if you will. My choice of words are challenging in the essence of simplicity, so please read carefully. I want you to see and read in my words that the real world isn't always "OBVIOUS" and is sometimes "ABSURD."

Only when you, the reader, see through the surface will you understand what is there. Take time to reflect on life, even if you don't really care.

Someday, you'll be older and wiser and see, or you'll still be traveling on some dull path with no binoculars to look through. I like to think that through doors of perception, you may find yourself.

If I could possibly simplify this observation, it would be just that ... simple. I feel that life is a mystery, almost a mystical magic show. Why not observe life as a mirage of the mind, yet with words having meaning and direction, not necessarily rhyme?

Surf through the illustrations and enjoy the real photos of family I have integrated and woven into my tapestry of short stories, Enlightments, Joyisms, and other stuff just tossed in! As you surf through, I implore you to enjoy riding your own "wild wave." See beyond the water because it's a kaleidoscope of beauty punctuated with a different view. Merely look through the surface and beyond the breakers! Imagine your own life through THE OPPOSITE END OF BINOCULARS!

The Power of the Pins

This is one of those inspiring "truths"—I would even say a miracle—to share with the reader, but that makes some too uncomfortable, so I'll will write it verbatim, exactly as I printed it in my journal on Dec. 23, 1996.

I was still living in Jacksonville, North Carolina on Vernon Drive and in the midst of a move to Johnson City, Tennessee. The massive undertaking was the remaining scraps of clean-up from the turbulence of losing my life as I knew it and all that entails!

Upon bringing my mama's old wooden jewelry chest into the house, I proceeded to dump out all the costume jewelry to clean and bring up happy memories during a dark period in my life and my first Christmas alone and lonely.

At the bottom of the dirty, mildewed pile of treasures laid a small brooch unfamiliar to me as relating it to Mama and her well-groomed wardrobe, always complete with her choice of accessories—jewelry in particular. After cleaning and brushing all the "found treasures," I took special notice of the little brooch, about 1 inch in length, with topaz rhinestones for eyes (one eye missing) and topaz inlay on the little crown this little angel wore. Although topaz is my birthstone, I never cared for the golden yellow color, so I never received a topaz piece of jewelry for a gift (except at the age of 4, when Barb bought me a set).

I continued to piddle in stuff, feeling overwhelmed by the magnitude of the cleaning, packing, and moving, more overwhelmed in the sense of being useless and worthless! I was in the small bathroom and decided to fix the drawer front that fell off with the slightest tug. In order to do this right, I put my arm into this mass collection of hair accessories, mismatched earrings, coins, etc. and pulled the contents forward, just allowing it to fall into a heap on the carpet. The one item that hit the floor was a bright gold little brooch with one missing topaz eye and inlaid topaz adorning the little angel's crown about 1 inch in length!

I sat back against the wall and turned the overhead light on for a better look. I was actually afraid to touch the little angel brooch! It is a feeling of disbelief, and you look around like someone is going to exclaim for you! This little angel pin was identical to the one I had just cleaned, and when I was able to stand, confused, as I made my way all the way to the kitchen, I looked at the first angel lying on the towel. Then, I made the trip back to the small bath again, looked at the bright gold angel pin still lying on the floor, and repeated this same trip to check on the first angel again. It was as though rational thinking ceased, grew confused, then awed.

On my third trip of verification, I finally brought the pin from the towel in the kitchen, laid them side by side, and stared at them still in disbelief! Being a person of tears for quite a while, I wasn't prepared for the "happy tears" that started. This possibility of my own little personal Christmas miracle was quite an experience for someone my age, a true Christmas, and the greatest gift I've yet received. These icons were so needed in the dark hole of a hardened heart and broken soul. Although tough times were ahead as I "blew in the wind," I had the little angel to look at and remember on Dec. 23, 1996, at 3:20 a.m.

The little angel that was in the wooden box had been stored in one of Michelle's boxes in the garage. We had gone through two hurricanes (Bertha & Fran). With the moisture that had come from these, everything had mildewed, and the cardboard box that contained the wooden jewelry box was located at the back bottom of her several boxes! The two were identical with the exception of the one retrieved from the garage, which had apparently reflected weathered damage and was missing a topaz eye, whereas the second one from the drawer appeared to be brand new, with the exception of one missing topaz eye!

How Do I Write in a Whisper?

This story of tribute is from soul to thought. This story is a heart sighing. This story could be a hymn, or it could be a Psalm! Without a doubt, it is a story of *true love: a story forever young*, stoically sitting and gathering dust, silent and patiently waiting as I lived life.

My personal *vaults* have been double locked and secured in that distant and farthermost chamber of the heart, placed there when my age could be counted in months instead of years at an age of tender feelings and emotions that had barely blossomed.

We all reach an age of comfort and wisdom when we can share an incredibly special, personal, and sincere love story. This does not overshadow *loves we now have*; it merely serves to enforce the sincerity of youth.

The need to take a mental stroll through one's personal memory log of long ago deems the need to also observe the *jagged edges and scars* of other hurts and losses—those that come with living and growing older. This is not an easy journey when strolling through almost four decades of memory. The cracks and crevices left by heartaches and heartbreaks, the forever loss of loved ones, remembering the longest trip ever taken at the grave site of a parent or child. This, too, is such a humbling venture.

When I reached the shelf of such an obscure private memory, I dusted the cobwebs of time from those contents to review them once again.

There was a feeling of deep friendship, shared ideas, and observations of life through youthful eyes and young emotions.

How do I write in a whisper? Such *a sonnet of the heart* that has intertwined with others' lives, those contributing composers who have earned the right to hear this long-standing sweet youthful sonnet will do so with their own personal tone and pace.

It is with sincere love for a *young man, forever young in memory*, that I quietly return this vintage safe deposit box to its rightful place, with closure and a gentle whisper of my own heart.

In Memory of:
Ronald Bruce "Ronnie" Gardner

The Hill

Coming off of Rhode Island Avenue in Bristol, Virginia, the famous Columbia Avenue hill jutted with an incline that rivaled any skiing locale. Walking down the hill, the first dwelling was on the right, that of the Almanys (their house burned in 1959). Mary Almany was my babysitter during school years when I only went half a day in the first grade.

The next house was the home of the Coxes. Their front door faced the side lot of the Almanys. Next was a small-framed rental house which had a variety of tenants. Directly across from the rental house on the left was another rental.

I recall the Herds, and in some fuzzy memory bank of mine, another family with two toddlers and an infant. I recall this only because I pinched the baby just so he/she would cry, and I could hold it. At some point, that house was razed. There were also two abandoned, weathered houses located parallel to our driveway, which I so dubbed, "House on Haunted Hill." Directly across from 120 Columbia Avenue lived the Heltons.

That was the total occupancy of the entire Avenue. The traffic coming off the hill consisted of, for the most part, dump trucks from the rock quarry or someone lost. I remember once at 6 or 7 years of age devising a plan—more like a ploy, a childish curiosity for the ultimate thrill of the week!

That was my problem, always needing to push the limit. So, I guess the term "extreme cycling" was my brainchild! On a chosen weekday, before anyone came home from school, ole Joy pushed that rickety red tricycle to the very top of Columbia Avenue hill, stood on the back foot plate, gripped those handlebars, and let the catapult effect take charge. With no sense of danger or hesitation, I was NASCAR at its earliest, smitten and watching the warp speed of those peddles rotating so fast they were a blur. I recall the trike eased right into our driveway, stopped, and elation was mine!

The memory of whether I shared that event with anyone escapes me. Being a petulant little brat, surely that accomplishment didn't escape my bragging opportunity. By design and law of physics, negotiating the curve should have been impossible. Considering the vehicle of choice and a featherweight novice child at the helm, a certain slingshot effect was a guarantee! The curve on Columbia Avenue had been the contributor of several bike wrecks, and cars too, miscalculating the angle of "dead man's curve" and ending up in the ditch line or greeting the huge Sycamore trees.

I recall a young teen girl biking had encountered tragedy at the curve. It is vivid because Mama went to her aid after Cotton Cox summoned the ambulance, and showing up was my excitement for that particular week! Being that I attest to spiritual guardians ensuring safety of little children, I envision these entities working in "shifts" and overtime at the Smith household. I have a theory of the guidelines God put forth qualifying under the "divine intervention clause." I think under some paragraph subtopic, it states, "If the human's age can be counted in months rather than days, ye shall intervene."

In all fairness, the hill had a positive quality. It served as a "winter carnival" for sleigh riders near and far due to the use of flat barrel lids, rubber inner tubes, cardboard, anything that would serve as transport for a thrilling slide down the hill! Again, the curve presented an obstacle for miscalculation!

Daddy had the solution. He supplied materials for a bonfire, strategically burning in the casualty line of miscalculation of the curve. At least there was a choice—ditch line or burn! So, I say Daddy escalated and quickened the learning experience of kids. After all, he himself had the innate qualities of "kidhood," and his thought process paralleled mine when I chose to take that tricycle down that hill! NO SENSE OF DANGER!

I'm How Old?

"Vanity, thy name is woman." Appropriate for the reality check I am getting ready to SLAP you with!

I did something so stupid—one of those actions that make you feel as though an entire year's worth of stupid attacks were used up in one fail swoop! I allowed adequate pity time, then said to myself, "SELF," this is too funny to enjoy alone! So, for all those around or about my age (52), NEVER LOOK INTO A FULL-LENGTH MIRROR WHEN NAKED!

There isn't one inch of my body that doesn't qualify under one or more of the following *adjectives*: bent, banged, folds, drapes, squints, sags, swags, droops, dimples, dangles, sways, swings, stretched, strained, scarred, crinkles, flaps, flops, bends, doglegs, thinned, thickened, spotted, barbed(?), bellowed, puckers, and probably stumped and stemmed should be included; might as well throw in pinged and ponged, winken-blinken, and nod! The days of picture taking on "my good side" are non-existent!

The days of sucking in and sticking out assets ARE OVER! As I look at my hands, the question is, "When did I get my Mama's hands?" I failed to remember that as the years zip-a-dee-doo-dah along, the skin goes along for the ride, the muscles decide on their own "hang down strike" with our bones and joints "swelling" support! The latest statistics show that four billion dollars are spent annually on cosmetics, all of which promise youthful appearance or a sort of magic potion to recapture what is lost or conceal what is there! HA! That is for the delusional, desperate, or fulfills that need for wishful thinking! At least product packaging is appealing—color coordinated to your personal décor—and flaunts titles that conjure up eternal youth.

I am gonna give out some information for free! Wood putty, duct tape, handy-wrap, paper clips, bungee cords, tacks, heavy starch, acrylic paint, polyurethane spray (non-gloss), sisal rope, perma-markers, Elmer's glue, toothpicks, and Papier-Mache. Start with these inexpensive supplies. Hey, it's up to your personal need as to "what to use where," or continue to grab for the illusive pipe dream which cosmetic companies convince you is the certainty of youth!

Four billion bucks! I changed my mind. Send me a dollar for "placement ideals" of sisal rope and paper clips, and if you believe that, well, send me $100 for the "non-profit" mirror removal movement. It's totally taxable, but I will send you a colorful framed print of…well, of something!

Age and Time

I have become that person "I Used to Make Fun Of." You know, "That One!" The eccentric who annually floats to the "surface of the gene pool" to share all the unsolicited sappy personal "Stuff" as though the recipients are waiting with Christmas glee and bated breath!

If I wanted to remind one and all of "age and time," I could elaborate on my two grown children and four grandchildren! In immediate residence are the following: Keith, my buddy and husband (he not only tolerates my quirks, but also he encourages them), two anti-social Scotties, one overweight cat, and a delusional four-year-old squirrel which I bottle fed. (He now knocks on our back door for meals.)

I wish to share a different view of Christmas. As I dust out the cobwebs of my "memory library" of family and friends who so intertwined and influenced my adult life, holidays seem to amplify those "simple times." The funny little sharing and giving, a time when $3.00 was enough to buy one and all of something.

There are those in our "family tapestry" gone from sight, yet vivid in memory. In that respect, they have left a legacy of life in living their unique laugh, whistling li'l tunes, even down to mannerism unaware—those who will be forever ageless! Aren't we blessed to have shared even the smallest "whisper" of their lives within our tapestry?

The adult Joy has been so fortunate to have love and caring. In Spite of Myself at times, I thank all of you. I was looking at Mama's recipe for a chocolate pound cake (I still think something was left out). Soda is terrible to eat! Vinegar is bitter, yet with all mixed together, the finished product is wonderful!

Good or Bad, our lives are similar to a cake recipe! Merry Holidays, Happy Life.

A Wrinkle of Time

Daily, I glance at my personal history book. Often I "read" it with attention to detail and content, sometimes merely speed-glance the key points of interest, noting new additions to my work in progress.

I think everyone starts their history book around the same age, yet the manuscript of this ongoing publication remains vague.

Of my list of goals for life, I never listed "write a personal history book" called wrinkles of time! It should be apparent that the history book is actually my face, complete with illustrations! I've looked at other history volumes, including yours most likely! I've decided to give these "history" books (faces, if you will) the proper respect.

If you were to win the Olympic gold medal, would you toss it in a closet? Would you ask a stranger to take a much-coveted Oscar off your hands? For the most part, awards and decorations in any field of recognition have no monetary value, but they're merely a tangible icon—bragging rights, if you will—and presented to the recipient in view of thousands of people!

Well, why not accept our face as a "trophy of living?" Let's imagine a committee being in session reviewing such finalists in a quest for the award-winning "personal history book."

The area between these eyes is deeply etched with prominent squint lines, perhaps with the despair of family problems, that vigil with kids or grandkids during illness, the worry for those walking troublesome paths in their lives, the erratic lines on the forehead, deep and hard as carved granite! Accentuated with a couple of half-moon scars, and those chicken pox scars carried for decades. This speaks for the walk-through life this face has experienced—that death of a child, the loss of love from a spouse, the illness of a parent or parents, the car accident of a teenage child, the concern for endeavors, changes, challenges in life. Yes, and the wonderful long-ago bike wreck scar, complimented with the scar from a glass pane that should not have been there! All elements written on this forehead emits "wisdom." In the mouth region, well-earned lines develop. More frowns than smiles have gave in to a permanent scowl. Points off for this page of "history." Reviewing the eyes, those so called "happy folds" (aka crow's feet) seem to belong to the face of a person "born old"—a face that is difficult to read from those deep-souled eyes. Yet the burden of life tragedies is most certainly reflected, just as those fluid little bags that carry a rich history of broken heart, broken dreams, worries, sleepless nights, but a glimmer of little happy, so to speak. Adding to the life of this face, there is also personal neglect and abuse from years of laboring in the outdoor elements, as a growing family depended on this!

I have decided that my face is now an award-winning "personal history." I am not ashamed of the character it reflects. I am oblivious to the wrinkles, crinkles, gaps, indents, whatever develops as my "history book" continues! What an honor to carry your life story, so I will keep it clean, nourished, sometimes wear a dust jacket, as any prized book does. This history of mine may not always be perfect, but it is educational and personal, so I choose not to erase it with surgical precision procedures. Why destroy a prize-winning history? I'll merely leave it here in my "HALL OF WISDOM."

Stitched with Heartstrings

Well, I say that the stitches using your heart are not only the strongest, but also they carry the extra little tinsel strength of love, memory, and warmth!

When all these elements mesh, you have a quilt! I've yet to see an ugly one—some in need of TLC and appreciation, perhaps, but no ugly ones! The same amount of care, time, and love has gone into each! Grant you, none I have produced will ever be featured in "Homes & Gardens" magazine, yet the purpose and spirit stitched into my "little rags" will indeed serve as a remembrance and treasure, hopefully, that will bring warmth and pleasure long after I am gone!

After the Carnage and Chaos of Christmas and New Year's, His Train Was Late

As I often do after the carnage and chaos of Christmas and New Year's, I take time to reflect and absorb both the "present" and "past" Christmas times.

As I grow older, it is a lot more comfortable to think of "past" due to the fact that I am truly "lost" when it comes to gifting my grandchildren, more lost at the hi-tech vocabulary they impart when describing what their heart's desire is. I am blessed they are patient and gracious to thank me for "whatever."

This little tale isn't about the "present." I am going back to a bittersweet time, a period before I was even born.

I can only imagine the hardships of the depression-era children and the hopelessness of parents, a time when young children were called upon, expected to contribute to the total welfare of their family. A time in history when Christmas was just another day, no exuberance, no wishes, no expectations. My own Mother, at the age of 18, lost her mama in 1937, yet she kept her eight siblings together. I have been fortunate to meet so many folks who lived during that bleak period. They brandish the soul of gladiators, wearing it, living it!

Now, it seems that for several years I have been gifted with what I describe as "miracles of the season," or as I refer to it, "God winks." This year was extra special! Just as my mother lost her mama, there was a young boy I will call Johnny from the heartland of America, who also lost his mama when he was a mere toddler. He was to grow up with no true memory of a mother's love or touch, but with a house full of other children and a farm full of work!

I reach into a child's tender heart and understand the "wishes" unfulfilled, the hardened spirit for lack of "magic" and hope, the lack of glee that all children should have, especially during the Christmas season.

I think Johnny may have meandered through a Sears and Roebuck catalog of the early 1940s or admired a sparse selection of simple toys at the mercantile, with no expectations to ever have a special Christmas or own one of those toys. I also would expect there was the holy grail of toys during that time, the TRAIN SET!

I do think young Johnny secretly longed for such a prize.

Just as little boys grow up, they also grow away from the magic and excitement of unfulfilled wishes, filing away those hurts and disappointments in a faraway corner of their memory bank.

Johnny grew into a fine contributing adult, served his country with a stint in the Army, and finished college while working and raising a family. Johnny's path in life meandered and detoured through many life paths before I was fortunate enough to intersect with he and Susan, his devoted wife, fortunate to be not only a neighbor but also to find true friends.

When we moved to Jefferson Street, I would often see John working in his yard or taking a leisure walk through the neighborhood. He was a very unassuming gentleman and often gave a small acknowledging wave as he went by.

I will fast forward at this point—the events of family member losses, losing a home to fire, losing health, fighting for one's life. Well, these are events that stacked on John and Susan, yet the love and commitment to each other never wavered.

I don't exactly recall how I opened dialogue with the very demure Susan, and I'm sure there were times John wished this old Tennessee gal, with my brusque nature, would have stayed away from his gentile, true southern lady. I'm sure glad I didn't!

We have pretty much become extended family over the last few years. We've been through some rough "peaks and valleys" as life often throws us. We've shared hopes, tears, stories of our youth, and dreams shared "bowl surprise" (if you're family you know what that is), and John recalling his Army days always piqued my interest. He could regale the minute details. I especially enjoy the "rabbit on the rifle range" tale! (Rabbit survived.) His military stint was cut short by a disability, and his love of country and devotion to "honorable duty" was never questioned. I could sense the manner in which he presented that "time in life." I also sensed that Johnny, the boy, was still masking an unfulfilled loss and longing, camouflaged by 70+ years of living, walking through that broken glass of life struggles.

Being that I enjoy toys more than I have the right too, I also enjoy giving "symbolic appropriate" toys to adults. Forget that suggestion on the box of "age appropriate." After all, I still keep my ancient, haggard, wire-protruding teddy bear handy at all times! Sometimes I put one of my many goofy hats on the bear, but never have I dressed him in any of my eclectic inventory of costumes (he would get indignant.) With that being said, I just wanted "Johnny" to have something "special"—a train set. During one of my ventures, I saw the many boxes stacked of train sets—not the Lionel hundred-dollar sets, but mere plastic "symbolic," yet complete, with 11 feet of track, locomotive, and box cars. The kind that just wanted to bring a smile to the inner child who most certainly never had a life of privilege but grew to be a selfless man of giving and of loving his gentile Susan.

This is where the "God wink" blessed us all. The randomly chosen train locomotive had I.D. numbers, as trains do. However, what are the odds of that very number "6012" etched on John's train being the last four digits of his Army service number, this too a way to identify service members? The odds of that happening aren't important or amazing! To me, that was a gift back knowing that I HAD INDEED CHOSEN JOHN'S TRAIN!

Special thanks to John C. Clawson and Susan, my friends.

Where Did Autumn Fall?

It always seems to catch me off guard when I "have a story in me." Here it is, September 29, 2002. I attempt to do those FALL things. You know, burn off the garden, see if the flowers are dormant enough to collect seeds, sorta look around to see if it's time to appreciate the greenery changing into the vibrant flaming colors—all those nice things about Autumn that I perceive as the last "hurrah" of nature before dozing into a winter slumber, somewhat allowing the earth to become the warm comforter for next year's generation of spring splendor. The next rebirth of new life in nature.

Maybe it's because of my age or perhaps selective, muddled memory, but it seems to me that when I was an up-and-coming adult, Fall had already fell by late September! You know, the lightweight sweaters necessary as we walked (yes, children did walk to school) early in the mornings. The shadows were stretched like a Rip Van Winkle yawn, and the colors were ablaze! The proverbial chill was in the air, serving as a forewarning that winter was standing in line to make a cold entrance!

You know, as a child, there isn't a great appreciation of seasonal changes. Nature isn't exactly a priority, yet it did indeed serve as a barometer to gauge our agenda, such as school starting, Halloween, Thanksgiving, then the holy grail of the year—CHRISTMAS!

So much for the FALL OF MY YOUTH! Surely the diminish of an entire season did not happen in a year or two. I guess just because we go on with living life, changes in seasons again aren't a priority. I actually am ashamed to say that for a few years, I truly watched seasons through glass, either working indoors or driving with windows and windshields being your portal to changing seasons. Oh, I guess if we think of environmental changes, pollution, ozone depletion, black holes, and all those other technical reasons for loss of season indicators, we accept it because the professionals tell us to!

Well, as anyone bored enough to read this knows, I view life through the opposite end of binoculars and through a kaleidoscope. Why not? It inspires me to switch brain functions! Anyway, I think in reality, we humans are merely parasites—even a fungus—to the planet that was "rented" to us, a place clean, balanced for our survival needs, sufficient for growing nutrients, adequate fresh water. In other words, it is a "rental property" that could actually survive without us and most likely thrive better without miniscule, self-serving human beings that have added insult to injury by procreating. So, there is a continuum, changing what shouldn't be, rerouting natural waterways, literally moving mountains, sealing and suffocating with concrete and cement. To sum it up, "WE LOOT, BURN, and RAVAGE."

I sometimes wonder if we humans transmutated. In other words, did our parasitical little selves once reside on other "rental planets?" If so, I'm sure those too were destroyed by our ancestral atoms! Doesn't it seem odd that in such a vast universe, endless galaxies and places in the depth of space we can't even fathom, much less live long enough to research and discover, God made a conscience decision to flick a dust particle, call it Earth, and inhabit it with little parasites (yes, us) to see what we would do with it?

Well, in that respect, I guess we can blame God for not offering us a "spare" to replace this beautiful "rental" after we have completed all the destruction our short lives allow! But as I implied, this planet could indeed be "THE SPARE!"

No, I don't profess to be an advocate of Greenpeace. I don't agree with those who try to save a tree by spiking it. I'm not a fan of Jules Verne or Edgar Cayce, not even Nostradamus. I just viewed the lack of changing seasons and got too carried away. As usual, I looked through those binoculars a little too long! All this observation because I grieve for real seasonal changes. I think that as October is within days, the temperature should not have a heat index of 94 degrees!

Still, I do admire Rachel Carson. She was so Avant Garde. I am proud of myself for writing a story about "Tommy Turtle and Goldie Goldfish" and having all that concern for pollution as an 8-year-old! Although the librarian Mrs. Sheets posted my story and gave me bragging rights, it was still based on "fantasy" and the "imagination" of a child. It's too bad that children under the age of 10 weren't caretakers of our planet. Imagine the possibilities! We probably would enjoy four definitive seasons vs. the two seasons we now have, "January" and "Dante's Inferno." I think I need to cut some more fresh flowers to bring into the house and leave all the serious thinking to those self-proclaimed professionals! Besides, it's too hot to enjoy being outside and getting sunburned.

A Special Person Came Knocking

This is the typed version of the attached personal note written inside the card I sent to Beth BEFORE she was born:

This week, a very special person came knocking on my heart. Although we haven't met, you are forethought in my thoughts because you are the beginning of a new stage in my life. You are blessed with a father with more love and desire for "his own" little child than you will ever know, as he still possesses a "child within" himself to make your formative years fun. ☺

Your Mom is still a stranger to me, but by mere choice of your Dad, I love her, and in our conversations, I hear the love in her voice for your Dad and for you.

You, little one, have a heavy title to carry... "the first." You will always have that title and the benefits it carries. ☺

I see a happy little person coming into my life to give me much needed laughter, many happy times, and memories. These are very extra special to me, things I thought I would never experience.

You have taken a part of my heart—It is now yours forever.

Your Grandmother

Pure Joy's Life Through the Wrong End of My Binoculars

A Wish for My Son

I wish my son "The Golden Child" a VERY happy birthday! I have a mom's view of my golden child!

NO, you do not radiate an aura of gold. However, you do have a heart of gold!

YES, you are admired by many people past and present because you have been with people when they needed help the most! You have saved lives and comforted broken hearts. That strength you have is unforgettable.

NO, you do not praise what you do in your career on a podium. You are a natural protector, empathizer, and genuine in your talents. YES, you were born to serve and protect.

NO, you don't love "loud," but intense, no more than you "hurt loud." That, too, is intense! YES, autonomy and interdependence is "so yours"—always has been!

NO, I do not grieve for my golden child when he is walking through "broken glass of life." I have faith you will not allow anyone to dangle your boots while you stroll through! I have watched you pick yourself up from the lowest valleys. YOU did it. YOU earned the bragging rights that you keep so private.

So, HAPPY NAVAL DAY, my GOLDEN BOY. Bradley, you are your mama's pride. (2006)

Bradley Stewart Fleenor was my greatest loss on December 20, 2021, when he died at the age of 52 from COVID-19.

Love of a Scottie

I can remember exactly when I fell in love with Scottish terriers! Long ago, when the little golden books were a whopping 15 cents, the back cover was lined with several animals. Right at the top middle was pictured the most beautiful little black dog I had ever seen! I can remember wondering if his hair really grew in that well-groomed, blocked shape. Over the years, many dogs came into my life, some by choice and others through enticement. Unlike other children dragging animals home, I kept mine and took responsibility! If pushed, I could probably recall every dog, cat, baby rabbit, field mouse, baby bird, etc., that came into my life, and certainly recall the heartbreak at the loss of my animals.

I ran across a real live Scottish terrier as an adult! Andy Marcy was his name! He was the pet of a neighbor, and when my neighbor suffered a heart attack, it was a pleasure to care for Andy. It was much later that ownership of a Scott was mine, although Brad and Michelle were quite young. It was their encouragement that pushed me to pay a grand total of 65 dollars for our first baby Scottie. Of course, his name had to be "Andy," and I have to admit that "Adult Joy" wanted that fuzzy, little black ball of energy more so than the children!

Now that I've established how long the desire for a Scottie had existed, I need to continue with the Scottie saga. "Randolph Scott" was our pet through the kids' junior high and high school years. This was followed by "Micki McGhee." The heartbreak of adopting out Micki is still a sensitive situation, but the adoption was my first experience with a "Scottie Rescue" program. The lifestyle and schedule would not be fair to her, so, with a heavy heart, I let her go.

If you have ever loved a Scott, you'll understand why so many years pass after the loss of one before you ponder ownership again! Five years of a new life, new lifestyle, less dependency of others in the household, and married to a wonderful man capable of patience, tolerance, and love of the precocious Scottie personality. I begin to meander on the internet.

Looking at Scottie pictures and reading biographies of Scotties in need of a home, I was amazed at the stringent guidelines and paperwork involved just to see if one would fit the "personality profile" for Scottie Ownership. I still don't recall the details of exactly when the e-mail came from Ginger McAfee, the Tennessee rescue "angel" we have.

A Scott for you! Wow! As I stated, being married to my kindred spirit, there wasn't a need for "permission." It was just understood! The need to travel to pick up our beautiful "Shelby" in October 2001 was no problem. Keith presented no reservations at Scottie ownership. Little did I know, Shelby was from the get-go—"Keith's girl." That was never in the "plan," but to see Keith enjoy Shelby and Shelby to display absolute thrill when she was with him was okay. I knew enough about snotty Scotties to accept her loyalty to him. That's not to say I didn't pout, but I kept it to myself.

Our beautiful black Scott settled into household routine. Her tolerance for me was acceptable. Her mainstay in life was to "look for" or "wait on" Keith! I finally had the opportunity to be a "house mom," to pretty much do "whatever." I accepted that bonding with Shelby was to never be. In the back of my mind, I heard Brian Bowers statement, "Well, Aunt Joy, guess you'll have to get you another one just for you." Although that was in jest, I again went to the rescue network, asking for the impossible. "Ginger, if you run across a wheaten Scottie, would you consider us for adoptive owners?" I thought that would satisfy my curiosity because a wheaten just "doesn't happen." Few and far between do wheaten Scotts become available! Within three months, we were asked if we wanted this little pitiful wheaten Scottie rescued from streets of Memphis. Mr. Bobbie MaGee gained love and pride back with us, and we received many lessons from him in return, especially Keith being educated to the fact that Bobbie was gonna snarl you away from your own bed if I was already in it. I too had my share of Bobbie's "fight or flight" responses many times and a few scars to show for it! We truly loved him the rest of his life.

May/December Love Story

I am telling this love story from personal observation and with great respect for two individuals who truly see the inner soul.

A year or so ago, it was obvious to me there was an extra spark in the old boy when a certain vivacious younger lady was seen passing by his house. He was in the autumn of life, distinguished, well groomed, and bearded with chestnut eyes of which reflected. Though he was born of good pedigree, his life had not always been kind, physically or emotionally. This made for "issues" in relationship development, so he kept his social circle small with guarded mistrust of pretty much everyone.

She, on the other hand, was vivacious, athletic, energetic, sporting a sleek figure with chestnut eyes and a "perma-grin" to anyone she met! This young lady exuded pure excitement and open-armed love, jumping at the chance to make new friends. I was taken aback at the ease in which he allowed her to approach him. Although he held his guard up, she was determined to meet and greet, opening a dialogue that only they understood.

Over time, he began to soften as he spent more time in her presence, even managing a half-snarled smile to others he met. Only "she" could bring out the best in this staunch, portly old boy! She made him feel "young and revived his soul," healing emotional scars he had worn like an old coat.

The unquestionable dialogue of love was there, but it also was a symbiotic love between two friends of very different backgrounds and certainly different energy levels!

As friendships developed, so did trust and relationships which allowed for her to stay weekends at his residence with nothing more than a platonic friendship and dogged conversation! Even the old boy's spinster sister (Ms. Shelby) tolerated the young lady, allowing her to interact with the other family members with minimal malcontent.

Their relationship is a love others could never understand or enjoy! A love of just being in each other's company, a love of "ages coming together," of non-judgmental, physical differences being of no consequence, no expectations aside from just the enjoyment of being with each other. Thus, as this May/December relationship continues, we should all take lesson from these two! There should be no conditions put on love, no "score card," no time limits, no demands, just honored to be with each other and enjoying the love and friendship and occasional dinner together.

Tribute to Bobby McGee and Abby!
An older Scottie in love with a young Jack Russell Terrier.

Treat Me Like a Dog Please!

Well, the title should not surprise those who are subjected to my view of LIFE and life lessons. So, take a look through the opposite end of my binoculars as I share another profound observation Bobbie Magee shared with me today!

The bath process for Bobbie is viewed as a communal activity; I'm right in there with him! As always, there's the wet-down, ensuring water is never poured over his head. I keep doggie washcloths and use the gentle touch cloth you'd use for a baby.

The pervasive scarring, nicks, and other maladies of what lay under his now beautiful Scottie coat seem to magnify as I really looked at the trauma of his past! As usual, I get blindsided by running a parallel visual through my mind when I least expect it!

FACADE, a condition I too have worn like a costume and mask more than I like to admit.

Bobbie Magee is indeed a "beautiful little boy," well groomed, well fed, regular health checkups, and well loved. Yet his emotional baggage is apparent, and trust—well, that is still in question at times, but his devotion to us is rock solid. I guess summing it up in a word, he has "issues" just as we humans tote around during times and events in our lives. Why do we feel it necessary to put forth a mask of delight when there is despair in our very soul?

Why clothe ourselves in garments too expensive, live in a dwelling that isn't a "home," and be enslaved to "stuff and status?" Bobbie, of course, was a "rescue" pedigree dog, a term we should be able to use when the Facade is too much. RESCUE ME. I strip off the veneer of perfection just as Bobbie Magee was stripped of his matted mottled hair. Be humble to your needs just as Bobbie was when sick and emaciated with a broken spirit and bruised soul.

I'm sure this parallel isn't for everyone to understand. There were times in my life (not so long ago) I should have barked "rescue me" instead of just aimlessly barking! Times I should have said, "I'm fashionably thin because I'm hungry! I'm lost just trying to survive!" Times that, for no reason other than burdens of the soul, I too would snap loud and mean because of fear.

I'm comfortable within myself and know and accept my personal shortcomings, yet just as Bobbie enjoys his "one true friend" (Shelby, our other rescue Scottie), I enjoy and trust being with the friend I married. He allows me to show my personal shortcomings, fears, and other "issues" just as Shelby allows Bobbie to grab her leash in his mouth and vent his fears by shaking and jerking her! Be a friend to someone with "issues." If you look close enough, you too will see the scars, nicks, and maladies that are covered with a mask of "I'm fantastic," even when their snap is loud and mean. It often means, "RESCUE ME!"

Dedicated to:
ALL RESCUE ANGELS!
Tennessee Scottie Rescue

I Miss Having Sciuridae

Well, there you go, thinking I long for some itchy, scabby disease! I would say to look it up, and you'll never forget it (that's what I always told my grands about a word), but it's simply because I miss raising orphaned baby squirrels.

In North Carolina, after hurricanes, there were so many baby squirrels from newborn to a few weeks old. I had no problem keeping them all warm and fed until they could be free or one became a pet for a friend. In South Carolina, the first very memorable baby was Rocko. His eyes were just barely open, so here I go feeding him the kitten formula and insuring he's warm inside my bra for a week or so. He then graduated to a fuzzy sock and baby blanket. Rocko always smelled like Downy fabric softener.

Keith called my attention to the fact that Rocko was ready to be free. I plotted on how to mark him so he would stand out. Being a pretty well-versed adult, I have not a clue why I attempted the next maneuver. Rocko and I went into the bathroom, I closed the door, and proceeded to put the red hair dye on his tail. Lawdy! Panic set in, his tail started swinging, and red dye was slung from ceiling to floor, and those lovely pastel shower curtains were destroyed. I sported muted tones of red on my face and arms for a week or so.

Well, after that epic fail and clean up, Rocko was treated to some pecans and a rest in his cage. The day of freedom came! I walked forlorn out to the largest tree and kissed Rocko goodbye. He never looked back.

The following evening, we experienced one of those heaven-busting summer storms with thunder, lightning and torrential rain. I grabbed the umbrella, running to the tree and yelling for my baby Rocko, and that wet little rodent jumped on my shoulder so fast I fell back, soaking wet and a bit dirty. We made our way back to the patio where we toweled off and I promised to let him decide when to leave the safety of hearth and home, which was the next day after the storm.

I'm pretty sure the grown squirrel that would thump the bottom of the storm door was my Rocko wanting some pecans. I obliged.

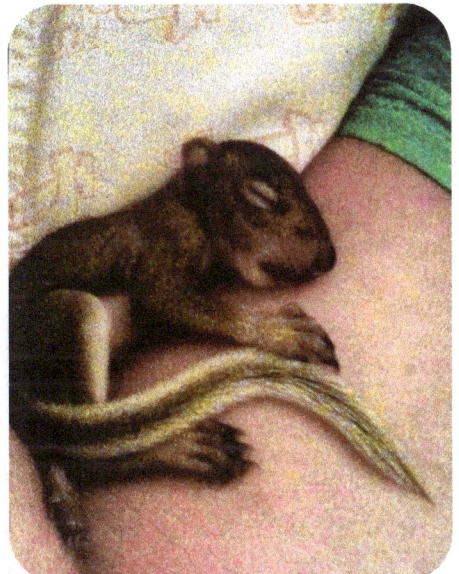 

My Life Heroes

I wandered off into that realm of my brain considered abstract in thought process, and I contemplated what a hero/heroine actually was. I think that, throughout life, we have layers of heroes—those which come and go, and some more memorable and impacting than others. A normal hero to a kid is most likely a police officer, fireman, cowboy, soldier, and not shunning Mom or Dad. Keep in mind that parents are tagged "role model."

My first kidhood hero would probably be Dancing Bear, a costumed person on Captain Kangaroo, followed by Mighty Mouse—yes, the cartoon. Emma Russell had a brother-in-law (John?). I considered him a grown-up kid...Not sure if that classifies as a hero. I also admired Doris Worley and Edwina Feathers, members of King Memorial Church. I thought they were beautiful ladies, yet not heroines. Mrs. Tester and Nora Riley were among my favorites, but as Sunday school teachers, they were not of hero caliber. I think I need to give this more thought! I can speak as a 52-year-old to my heroes/heroines outside of family. Garbage pick-up personnel are heroes to me, and veterinarians are top-notch heroes. Of course, those involved in any animal rescue are, without a doubt, heroes in my eyes! Thanks, Tennessee Scottie Rescue.

Okay, let me be honest here! Heroes and Heroines receive recognition, medals, etc. That is okay; we all need the encouragement of fellow humans' undertakings and achievements to motivate us and give us hope that there is good in the world! Well, I salute the ones we never hear about, never public as to their actions or reactions—the "silent majority." When I question the "good will" of mankind, this is my positive thought process attesting to the fact that "THE GREATEST DEEDS ARE THE ONES WE KNOW NOTHING ABOUT." Wanna be a hero?

Good for you, and just think—you never have need to prove it!

Greatness for Something-or-Another

Come on! Admit it. You know we all desire a degree of greatness! Personally, I envision my own greatness while I'm living, thus I feign humbleness as I toss out one of those Southernese "Aw shucks!" statements while gloating inward.

I've considered "what if" the *Smithsonian Institute* requested my presence to recognize something-or-another affiliated to me. Oh, what a grandiose moment with elaborate pomp and circumstance. In reality there is a personal affiliation to the *Smith-Smithsonian*, our grand display being a vintage smokehouse, not the least grandiose, of true humble stature and no need for fanfare.

Within our Smith history, this structure *is* greatness.

Or if I was *graced* with *amazing* perfect-pitch singing, inundated with calls from stages and domes worldwide with, "Please, will you perform?" Reality is, I am related to a Grace, and she's pretty amazing, just as my affiliation to Will, and he certainly entertains and enlightens with his antics and performances. *Hey! I am their Great Aunt!* I think of the dream of achieving greatness by accomplishing an impossible task such as taking flight toward the sun for scientific purposes. In reality, I have a son who dared take flight in order to achieve his dream and accomplishments for all the right purposes! *What Mom would deny "that's greatness?"*

I lost my son, Brad, on 12-20-21. We all lost a great man.

A Palace from Pallets

I can't recall why I voiced my desire to have a playhouse! Somehow the request for one isn't as memorable to me as the process of how it came about!

Minnie voiced (on Columbia Ave.), "We had the whole house as our playhouse." That is so true!

Anyway, in the late summer of 1959, Daddy commenced to bring home the materials for this undertaking. Mind you, this was no small achievement! It wasn't as though he could run down to Home Depot and pick up all the materials. So, slowly, the wooden pallets were squirreled away down near the wild cherry tree.

My role in this "home development" was, for the most part, to stay underfoot (Southernese for "in the way").

As most children this age, I was egocentric and oblivious to the fact that this task added a few more hours to Daddy's workday! I remember well him sorting the planks as he dismantled the used wooden pallets, stacking just the right ones for the roof shingles of my palace! I'm sure that, for the sake of expedience, the floor was 4x4 (standard pallet size). This specification would equate to a very small closet. However, at this age, I was quite thin! Well, I could stand sideways, stick out my tongue, and look like a zipper. The wall height of my palace was also 4 ft., with one small window (by request). The door was finally complete, hinged with used rubber inner tubing (cars had inner tubes then).

Carpentry wasn't a strong point of Daddy's, but in the eyes of a little girl, he built two palaces—his first and last! That is some labor of love! Looking back on Daddy's personality, this "palace build" was as much for his pleasure as mine.

The pallet palace went from Columbia Ave. to the country, where it was placed on a little plot of real estate near the woodshed, embellished with a plastic windowpane and little white curtains! Oh, how I enjoyed the palace! And I think this is where I really developed my engineering skills with wood. After all, with the plentiful woodshed at the front door of my palace, I got creative.

As little girls do, I outgrew my palace, and it remained empty until it was once again moved back to town, where Eric, Mary Ellen, and Ed's German Shepherd used it as his doghouse. Being a pre-adolescent, my palace wasn't a priority or a treasure, so I don't know when or exactly where it was razed! Without a doubt, the memory of where it was raised and by whom is a treasured memory that will never need repairs! Thank you, Daddy!

FAMILY STORIES

"I Wish for You" With Love to My Grandchildren

I never knew how to make it better for my children! In fact, my actions, or lack of, probably made it worse for them when it came to "life lessons." Now that I am Fivey-O, the commonsense age, I present these wishes in the genuine spirit of love, hoping my grandchildren appreciate sage wisdom, and the fact that YOU ARE MY MONUMENT. I wish for you to visit a good memory of me, not a cold stone! Laugh at how I lived and loved you, and I will never be gone!

I really want you to know about "hand-me-downs" and the treasures to be found in thrift shops, about homemade food such as dilly bread, and to incorporate "bowl surprise" meals into your life. I wish for you to allow vanilla ice cream to serve as a milk substitute in cereal bowls. These things I really do!

I wish for you to learn HUMILITY by being humiliated and learn HONESTY by being cheated!

I wish for you to learn the task of housework in order TO HELP. I hope you not only clean up after yourself, but also quietly and without fanfare clean up after others!

I wish for you to learn the skill of cleaning a car, checking the oil, and changing a flat tire! I certainly hope you are not GIVEN a car at 16, but given a JOB to instill pride and discipline, which are skills you carry throughout life.

I wish for you to witness the birth of an animal and experience the pain of losing a pet!

I wish for you to "get your feelings hurt" when you take a stand for something you believe in. Stand by your conviction!

I wish for you to walk with your friends and do so in a town where you are safe.

I certainly hope you are not ashamed when Mom, Dad, or other adults involved in your life drop you off in FRONT of your school!

I wish for you to dig in the dirt for absolutely "no reason," to stomp a mud puddle dry "for your own reasons." I wish for you to appreciate and love reading books for MANY REASONS! Through reading, you have the freedom of travel and wonder as you enrich your creative ability and promote healthy imagination.

I wish for you to build and contribute to your memory bank of information and appreciate the awesome power of words!

I wish for you to continue adjusting to this hi-tech computer age yet learn to add and subtract in your head! I also wish for you to continue using a #2 pencil, and a big eraser!

I wish you the experience of "getting razzed" by your friends when you have your first puppy love crush! And for you NOT to razz those same friends when they experience the same!

I sure wish for you to talk to your parents, respect other adults, and not "TALK BACK." I wish you to know when you should TALK WITH your parents, and the knowledge of their UNCONDITIONAL LOVE regardless of what you say or do! This I wish you to experience and pass on.

I wish for you to skin your knees climbing a mountain and burn yourself at least once! I wish for you to get really sick when you try that first beer. If you try smoking, I sure hope you do not like it! If your friends offer "other" items to experience, that person is NOT YOUR FRIEND! Guilt loves to involve others!

I wish for you to remember that the mouth you eat with is the same mouth profanity and hurtful comments will contaminate! I wish for you to respect your body and keep in mind sex is not a casual game!

I wish for you to experience defeat, so you truly appreciate victory. I wish for you to lose a footrace at least once in your life, then congratulate the one who defeated you. You will appreciate disappointment. Set high goals!

I sure wish you appreciate and make time for grandparents and other older adults! Enjoy them, respect their knowledge, and express delight at stories repeated several times. I wish for you to KNOW you have the right to defy any adult when their words or actions are uncomfortable. KNOW you will NOT be in trouble by "telling on them," then GO TELL!

May you feel sorrow and grief at a funeral and feel the Joy of Holidays!

I wish for you to contribute—not contaminate—your planet.

These things I truly wish for you—tough times and disappointments, hard work, and true happiness!

I hope you learn the WORTH of a few things and the VALUE of everything, with the good sense to recognize the difference!

I wish you peace and inner serenity, spirituality, and faith. I wish you stability, comfort, and true love—both to give and receive! Make it happen!

Onnie: 1993, rewrite: 2000, rewrite: 2004
Here it is 18 years later in 2022, and it still applies.

Love y'all,
Onnie

Common Cents and Double Nickels

It seems that I get a little melancholy around birthdays. Within one week, four of the Smiths reach another pinnacle of aging, a combined total of 243 years!

I totally rely on family to inspire my pearls of wisdom—those Minnie enlightenments, Patty and her AUDIO handicap (I still appreciate constant humming), brother Luke's tinsel strength and Yoda humor. However, Barb (aka "Babba Dean") has yet to be recognized for her Zen qualities! I personally feel that I've been remiss, however she and I pretty much offer up "equal insult opportunities" and "pound some feathers flat" when necessary. We strive for truth yet love with a tenacity unequaled.

Well, as I try to validate my "slighted behavior," it can be summed up by finality of agreement by both parties! Each time I look through the "wrong end of my binoculars," I can imagine Barb reading my story or observation and spewing forth that contagious deep laugh. It must be our Daddy's genes that dictate the simplicity of profound philosophy and theory.

Paul Smith Sr. was a maze of complication possessing a labyrinth of single syllable English. Perhaps Barb and I were patient enough to process Daddy's myriad "grab bag" of wisdom!

For the most part, one had to "study on" many of his theories for a decade or so! Thus, by design, his philosophies pertained and became logical when one reached a certain age! The wonderful example of his "double nickel" year brought us a chuckle as she and I spoke fondly of Daddy "wearing that statement out" in those months leading up to his 55th birthday. I have to laugh at myself, for I too am at the "double nickel" year! I think I'll WEAR IT OUT myself.

Where's the Love?

I've done it again! As Keith and I walked into Minnie's kitchen, my mouth had a stupid attack. Minnie is a familiar sobriquet for Mary Ellen, my older sister of reliable stability.

I hope to validate the error of my tongue. I don't know if an apology is in order, but an explanation is.

There are certain expectations of "same stuff" being present. When I saw a "sterile" refrigerator stripped to bareness, I was taken aback! It isn't as if the trip to East Tennessee is a destination of "fridge worship." However, would it not shock you to walk into a library and find all the books gone or enter a museum and find all great works of art gone? *Point made!*

Minnie fails to realize that her fridge has ascended to a level of priceless vignette. It reflects fun events and births. It became a visual growth chart of her grandchildren, interjected with other family members interchangeable accordingly and silently evolving into a variable historical database at a glance. This fridge joins the ranks of "Smith-Smithsonian" status! A symbol, a respected chronicle of life.

Do I need to explain that I live vicariously through your eyes of Nana-dome? This is your destiny, you know! Minnie is the curator of history and current events, orator of great stories associated with those tacit illustrations and enhanced by works of crayon art so intertwined they harmonize like a sweet lilt sonnet.

I beg my sister to look through the wrong end of those magical binoculars! Besides, it was YOU voicing how little children "don't like change" in their comfort zones. As you well know, I'm skilled at using that Fischer-Price lobe of my brain!

Sure, you see a receptacle for cold milk and leftovers, a vault of "personal organization" (a zone where no one dares to tread). Nana notes a disheveled lid on the mayo, the cheese stack placed horizontal vs. vertical. Dare I say, an item on shelf #2 has been placed on shelf #3. I so envy this degree of organization and rotation. My fridge is best described as "box of surprises," however the front and sides are covered with photos, coupons, lists of "to-dos" and even more lists of "never gonna do." My displays serve more as dust covers. Minnie's serves as a gauge to current events, headliners, achievements, and overall a condensed, easy-to-read icon of "same stuff!"

It is only because of who she is that I go to this extreme. After all, if you really want to find out where the love is at Nana's, all you need do is step inside. It permeates throughout.

So, thanks Minnie/Nana for being a good sport, and if you run out of exhibit space in the kitchen, there's the fridge out in the garage!

A Tisket a Tasket – My Special Basket

We all enjoy receiving a gift basket. I think it transcends us back to kidhood, whereas quantity of "stuff" assured an altered state of euphoric bliss!

Special occasions, such as Christmas, birthdays, births, etc., dictate appropriate contents for gift baskets. At Christmas, you can expect .0001 oz jars of jellies, summer sausage, and some type of cheese imitator. Birthday basket contents are optional as to the interest of the recipient, and birth celebration baskets are pretty much self-explanatory!

I received the most wonderful basket in August 2003! It isn't the first I have received in my fivey two years, and hopefully not the last, yet I can't imagine getting one with so much meaning! You see, this was a "just cause" basket from Minnie and Patty. They both failed to realize exactly how much they stuffed in that 15-inch basket!

Obviously, the wonderful bags of Starbuck coffee beans took center stage. Patty made it a point to hand deliver this treat annually all the way from Seattle! With this gift, she was sharing her pride of product that provides her a living and also shared her YODA knowledge of coffee in general. So, you see, Patty gave me a "part of her day-to-day life" and enabled me to take full advantage of this by including a new Coffee Bean Grinder! Ain't that a hoot!

The pint of Tennessee honey was most significant. I admire symbolism, and I immediately knew this was representing my kidhood nickname "honeypot." GOD BLESS YOU! What a sweet reminder and a delicious memory.

The five packs of Juicy Fruit gum immediately conjured up how I swiped Mama's Juicy Fruit on a regular basis, especially at church on Sunday night! She probably insured it was available for that very reason—another delicious memory!

My cornhusk doll epitomizes Minnie—a little delicate-looking, but tough with the "starch" to take on the world.

Little did Minnie know she allowed me to share her love of a grandchild. Reece made sure his puppy sticker had a place of honor in the basket! Along with the li'l sticker was an honest, loving innocence, sincere in the very presentation and offering to Aunt Joy's basket. The very act of giving from a child is priceless! Thank you, sweet Reece. I have placed your beautiful sticker with the two buckeyes Hayden blessed me with three years ago.

All this nestled in a cushion of "sunshine" yellow! So, you see, dear sisters, the memories you gave back to me—the reminders, the sharing of life and love—are countless in my "just cause" basket. I love you.

Brother, Where Art Thou?

Yesterday, I received one of those calls we dread. Billy Wayne Smith had left us, and again my family tapestry suffered the type of tear that cannot be replaced. I always viewed Bill as one of those elusive relatives, darting in and out of my younger years similar to the flight of a hummingbird, quickly and with versatility yet with the blink of an eye could be off again with his style of "self-proclaimed pattern."

I am saddened that his lineage was lost before he came into the world, saddened that he relinquished to a plight chosen for him.

In my twenties, we had the opportunity to interact. Bill was an equal to my daring spirit and wild horse racing. I so enjoyed those early conversations and admired his "flight pattern" of ambition and experiences. Again, just as fleeting as the elusive hummingbird, our years and life patterns went separate ways without understanding.

It would be a decade later before I had the opportunity to look eye to eye with Bill again, sincerely stating, "We were kids and knew no different, but the adult Joy will never reject you as a brother." Only with a mere nod did he acknowledge that profound statement. 20 years later, he explained the depth of what that meant to hear from the "youngest" of the Smith kids.

In August of 2003, as we sat on his deck talking with each other, I had the sense of "weighing the man, not his title." We actually derived laughter from each other as we viewed our lineage through those somewhat "smeared windows" of choices made by others so long ago.

With benefit of computers, Bill and I communicated almost daily. Many times, we discussed a common ground too sensitive for others our overshadowing "nearest and dearest enemy" shared by brother and sister. We also shared a style of humor only friends are capable of! He could beat my feathers flat with his dry and quick retorts, yet we were of the same mind set when it came to our "gene pool," keeping chlorine close by at all times. We did so in the spirit of fun, laughter, and acceptance.

I find myself gently gathering shattered fragments of our conversations, pieces placed in my hall of wisdom, treasured and preserved forever. I smile at our ability to be comfortable with our "equal insult opportunities" and to savor our tranquility of "what was" without cynicism or judgement.

The fact that I lost the same brother twice isn't so. I truly lost a friend, and just as he lived, fleet in flight, so did he leave, swiftly and unassuming.

Goodbye, my brother my friend.
For: Bill Smith, Jan. 14, 2004
Written: Jan. 15, 2004

Her Secret Garden

Recently, I was fortunate enough to intersect with my niece, Jamie, and although we crossed paths a couple of years ago, it's been 30 plus years since our last conversation. Sweet Jamie had not changed much. Her heart got larger and softer, most likely brought about by the precious daughter and son she is so rightly proud of, and a husband who loves her unconditionally.

I don't recall how literature came into conversation, but Jamie shared that one of her favorite books was "The Secret Garden" by Frances Hodgeon Burnett. I couldn't help pondering this statement because I know Jamie's life was anything but smooth. She has traversed jagged edges in life, with claw marks on her very soul. I relate to this very well, but that's a different story

I gave lots of thought to the parallel of Mary Lennox, the 10-year-old character in this book, and that of Miss Jamie, who to me was always the child I remember. She would indeed relate to this book, as she too had created her own personal secret garden as she strolled through the paths of life, seeing the beauty that "could be" if she worked on it.

I'm pretty sure Jamie always had beautiful scenery in her thoughts, wanting her garden to be an escape and a vista of beauty—a place that would reflect the sonnet of her heart.

Miss Jamie still has a voice that's disarming and as soft as the heartbeat of a baby, the ability to sooth those in crisis, a supporting touch so reassuring to those fortunate enough to intersect with her personally or professionally.

Just as Mary Lennox was a victim of her own isolation, Jamie also had those periods in her life. I don't know at what point on her path Jamie pulled herself up and dusted off her knees, but I feel that her twenties were spent camouflaging her insecurities. I also think, at this time, she began to realize there was emptiness in her fears. She was simply tired of listening to the sound of her own tears.

During the time her own wall grew, she hoped no one knew where she was. Like Mary, she was somewhat a victim of her own isolation. Oh yes, there were a few lost dreams along the way, those times she experienced pain so deep she wondered why people didn't hear it!

Jamie had to grow strong so that her spirit would not wither and die as she experienced life lessons such as, sometimes, people leave you to fight alone. Jamie had forgot how to dance in the rain. It's common for people going through life's pain to merely lock their hearts and build a wall. In all chaotic beauty lies a wounded work of art.

To me, Jamie is truly a work of art reflecting love, a forgiving spirit with the compassion and desire to help others become the best they can be with what talents they possess.

We're all fortunate to have her, whether she graces you with her presence as an educator or just the sweet friend or family member she truly is. I know Jamie was nervous when she found her purpose, and as her walls became covered with the beauty of new beginnings for so many lives she touched, she forgot her isolation. A girl "in need" became a woman for "those in need."

So many of us hide behind our walls and refuse to see beauty only isolation. I'm so proud to know someone such as Jamie, so generous with her time in helping others see the future of beauty in their own garden, and self-sacrificing with her own talents to share. Jamie indeed doesn't see the golden rule as a suggestion. She has a love for the Lord and a spirit that reflects that love.

Thank you, Miss Jamie, for all you do, have done, and will be doing till your children follow your guidance and love long after you're gone! Don't "pack your bags." You have a lot more to do!

Jamie lost her battle with cancer in August 2020.

Daddy's (Ka Stroffs Ta Fee) Catastrophic Day

I guess after Mama passed in 1985, the only common link in residence at 414 Goodson St. for Daddy was the dual companion they had shared—old Friskie cat! This feline also had another well-deserved title—W.A., the first word being WILD! Frisk was the original "stealth fighter" combined with the tenacity of a WWF character. I'm sure Daddy had many tearful, private chats with Frisk; she was his best buddy! It is with both chuckles and tears that this little escapade is regaled, and if you know Daddy, it's easy to envision.

It was Daddy's next door neighbor to the house on Goodson Street sharing this with me. This neighbor was privy to seeing Daddy daily and quite accustomed to his eccentricities! It seems as though Daddy was making his usual walk around to the basement, hollering for Frisk, or as Daddy addressed her, "Frikkie-Brickki." As most of us know, Daddy was a "man of wardrobe comfort," and his idea of "changing wardrobe" appeared to be turning his T-shirt and boxer shorts inside out. Thus, it seems that Daddy was making prominent to Larry the worn condition of his boxers, accentuated with apparent skids! As Daddy apparently came back around toward the front walk, there in the road was a "Siamese cat casualty," and the wailing commenced! "OH, MY FRIKKI'S DEAD!" Steeped in true grief, Daddy apparently wanted to share his loss with his associates, making his way to the Ice Cream shop, approximately half a mile from the house and stopping at the café he frequented. We can only surmise how many folks were subjected to this sight of a rumpled, elderly man, lamenting to the very heavens as he held this quite stiff, mangled cat tenderly in his arms. Keep in mind his "wardrobe of comfort" (T-shirt and worn-out cotton boxers) as he made his way around, reaching out for comfort and consoling. It seems his last stop was to share his loss with his neighbor, the stiff, mangled cat still cradled in his arms! "MY FRIKKI BRIKKI IS DEAD!" The grief earnestly emitted from Daddy's very soul!

All of the sudden, I was told that Daddy went into a somewhat chortled laugh/cry, stating, "There's my Friskie!" as oblivious old Friskie came strolling up the sidewalk. Larry said that Daddy immediately threw down the carcass, which 10 seconds prior had been precious cargo, dismissed the "mistaken identity," and never looked back as he scooped up the very alive Friskie. He all but skipped back into the house, and most likely, Daddy fussed at her, kissed her even more. And, as usual, both arm and paw went to bed!

Keep in mind, Daddy walked his trip of grief, complete with wardrobe of comfort and a dead cat!

Blonde True Stories

As she zipped around town in her red sports car, one which complimented her beautiful blonde, flowing hair and bronze tan, a disaster struck!

Her flat tire was fixed by an eager young man, and he pointed out that the problem tire was quite worn. Being the blonde she was (there seems to be some cranial gray matter shift with the blonde gene), a thought crossed her mind: *Hey! My tires were advertised as "40,000-mile radials," and I've only driven 32,000 miles! Boy, am I going to take care of this!*

She makes a beeline to the poor tire dealer where Mom originally purchased her daughter's tires.

The scene wasn't nice. As you know, this "genetic trait" of blondedom also demands that *everything halts* until demands are met. The total disbelief and head scratching by the service department and management of the tire dealer served to heighten her indignation, so a phone call to the corporate office followed. *Ugh! Where's the sanity!* With sympathy for the poor manager of the local dealership, the blonde's mom decided to halt the madness (which she was accustomed to from such a child). A discrete phone call from Mom, along with a $98.00 check, resolved the issue (you would think). The manager was more than willing to call the blonde, asking her to bring in her car for a brand new tire and rotation.

Smugly, the young woman acknowledged that the justice she demanded was right and proper. Mom all but choked on her drink as her blonde daughter announced THE GRAND PLAN to get the remaining three tires replaced, using the same "blonde logic."

"I'll call the corporate guy in the morning and get that taken care of. The manager at the tire store doesn't wanna mess with me!"

I agree! He didn't!

– Mother of a beautiful, natural blonde daughter

* The color of the car and actual mileage have been changed (the young tire changer is just added for semblance of reality) to protect MYSELF from wrath of a certain blonde I know and love.

Michelle's Little Doll

I try to give you gifts of "need"—those things you deny yourself so Matthew can be his "wants."

This is a very different gift; it isn't yours to enjoy (yet). Rather, it has been such a delightful visual illustration of my little girl and provokes memories only I appreciate.

The defiant expression reminds me of your independent nature from early on. The somewhat rumpled cute pink is a reality of my baby girl, taking comfort over feminine any time! The golden crown of hair so envied. The time of your life I should have appreciated you more so.

Never forget, I loved you as my little girl, and I love you as my grown-up little girl. And if you ever doubt, take "Mimi" onto your lap. Hug her as I have so many times, and if you listen with your heart, she may share the many conversations we have had.

I love you so and trust you to care of your namesake, Mimi! Never forget that warm memories, not cold monuments, honor those you love and who love you unconditionally!

– *Mom*

Matthew's Little Big Miracle

Parents go to sacrificing lengths to insure their child experiences a memorable, special birthday! Nothing within limits is "too much" yet there are sometimes barriers to make wishful thinking impossible.

In the summer of 2002, Michelle was confronted with a quandary of providing not one, but two birthday cakes for her baby boy, Matthew, soon to celebrate his fourth birthday! With Matthew in preschool, it was expected that parents share a birthday party for all students, and certainly Matthew was to have his "home" celebration too, thus the need for two cakes.

Michelle, being the independent mom she is, insured that Matthew had his school sheet cake, complete with birthday treats for his entire class. I think this was the Batman cake, yet his birthday at home was another matter, being that her payday fell after his big day—a situation I certainly relate to!

We as parents desire to make it "special," especially for a little guy! When Keith and I made a trip to Shallotte for a birthday visit and delivery (Michelle and Matthew's birthdays fall within days of each other), she was sharing her little miracle that she had spoken to me about on the phone!

It seems that the different bakeries in their town donate items to the department Michelle is in charge of, the Council on Aging, State of N.C. As the gentleman making a "timely delivery" handed off the sheet cake to her, not only did this cake have another of Matthew's heroes, Spiderman, but—get this—also the cake said, "Happy Birthday, Matthew!"

What are the odds of that? Michelle was shocked but expressed her delight at experiencing a positive in the midst of lots of negatives taking place in her life—some of which she thinks I'm not aware of.

Just another fine example of "God works in mysterious ways." I'm so proud of her and wish her more little miracles throughout her life.

There's My Star

I always know where to find my brilliant star, her light so
Tightly woven, it joins us at the soul.
I tilt my head with open eyes, it is not into the night I gaze
I look into the now and then, I look into her face.

Stars often wan and waiver, exploring other skies,
My star,
Has often sought to hide in shadows, yet never left my heart,
Or the sight of Mama's eyes.

Her twinkle may diminish but never goes away,
She can't hide,
A brightness born within her,
She can't hide the secrets of our souls.

My star shined when opaque fog surrounded life,
My star pierced darkness with her silent song of hope,
My star brought the sunshine back to Mama's soul.

She is a star of wonder, a star of very bright,

I wish upon her to never lose her "song of every night."

When my little star is burdened and hurt surrounds her night,

When she has lost her "Waltz of Life,"

When silence has invaded,

She merely needs stillness to hear her Mama whisper.

You are always and forever my baby; I will always be your guiding star.
Happy Mother's Day, Sweetheart, I love you more than life.

Eulogies of Life

I think it's this season of loss that prompts me to consider eulogies and epitaphs. Winter months certainly peak the percentage column of "personal loss" within my tapestry of family. Last week was my first loss of a sibling! I'm going to quote from my "tribute to family" story about Bill.

"Bill, the elusive stranger. Thank you, Bill, for allowing a little Joy see her first Asian American lady seated in our living room; and you sporting a curious uniform of pure white, my first sight of a Navy man. Thank you for a challenging horse race when you, Barb, and I enjoyed Sunday outings at Ft. Campbell. Thank you for the look of 'it's okay' when I expressed that the adult Joy will never deny you. Thanks for teaching a strong lesson in life just by being Bill Smith." Nothing more need be said.

Losing the first in my generation reminds me that "I'm closer to the end than to the beginning." That isn't a frightful observation. I am over 50! I have walked in the shadow of death and made it through. I'm thankful for healthy children and grandchildren. I've watched another brother lose his heart's song by the unimaginable task of burying his own child. I've also observed that those tender, pain-filled places in his broken heart and soul eased with the soft whisper of summer's song. Robin Smith-Brooks truly did live and left behind her personal "GREATEST LOVE STORY"—such an awesome legacy, such a humbling gift.

Like all families, we have suffered losses, trials, and tribulations that "test the fiber" of love and friendship, and just as family units have that "eccentric" relative (you know, that one observing life through the wrong end of binoculars), I, by self-admission, qualify as "that one."

We can't take life seriously cause none of us get out alive!

I think that about 25% of what I write tells 100% of what I don't! Now, ponder that meaning! I have always tried to follow the rules at least once. Walking to the beat of my own drum usually had a miserable outcome, so when the age of "common sense" and honest faith slammed me face down, the only place I could look was up!

When we ignore that tap on our soul, then the thump usually gets our attention. I speak of DO-OVERS in life. I finally realized we have DO-OVERS! It's our children! They don't do it right either, so that's why *they* have children! Thus, the continuum.

This is where eulogies and epitaphs come into play. Have you ever wondered about your own? Ever thought how it would be to hear loved ones and friends express it? Well, being the eccentric one, I've made a serious decision! I'm not only going to write my own, but also for those I love and care about.

There is no disrespect intended, merely a style of writing and healing at my personal sense of loss. After all, wouldn't you rather be able to hear all those comments while in the flesh? That allows for editing rights (and litigation). Unless I drop dead today, there should be additions to my own "praises." Guess I need to end my personally written eulogy with "fill in the blanks." Have fun with it!

Things That Make Ya Go HUMMMMMMMMMM

Have you ever given thought to the very act of humming? Why does someone hum? What could possibly provoke the subconscious to connect to our audio equipment, travel through neurons, nerves, and all that it takes in our communication skills to drone out such a sound, so often to the point of being distracting or a nuisance to others?

If you check the official definition of "hum," it means to sing a tune without opening the lips or articulating words. Also, it's used to indicate hesitation, displeasure, or surprise. Well, if you dissect the definition, I guess that singing without articulating words COULD get on someone's nerves! We are not a society of acceptance to such! This is an unexpected act to most people who indeed are more receptive to moan, groan, bitching—just in general "a sense of brow beating, downgrading." So, how dare someone emit an uplifting sound? How dare an individual murk up a workplace with this "perky, often subconscious gesture?"

Again, it is, for the most part, family which inspires me to observe life actions through the "opposite end of my binoculars," so thanks to Patty. Again, I reviewed, analyzed, and soul searched as to why some of us hum. YES, I HAVE DONE SO FOR YEARS! Or drone out a low whistle. You know, Trish, folks should be more appreciative! We can't possibly be happy and carefree during the entire timeframe of our constant humming or whistling!

I think the solution will suit everyone! Continue what we do naturally. With the most serious facial expression, inform all that this malady is a form of "TOURETTE SYNDROME," although we have trained ourselves to replace the uncontrolled profanity associated with this condition to the low, constant, uplifting hum!

Hey, Patty, they will THANK YOU for your consideration and hard years of training

Hum on, sister!

Our Smith-Sonian Smokehouse

In the winter of 2000, I managed to capture a real piece of Smith history as I photographed, among other structures, the smokehouse located "in the country!"

I'm not sure when the smokehouse was built, but I do know that there are pictures of a much younger Gramps, Grandma, and Jady taken in that locale. As an educated guess, I would say it was built anywhere from 1925-1930.

Even when the smell of fresh wood emitted from this little building of service, she was no beauty! The design is somewhere between a lean-to and a shanty—yet accommodating for the purpose of "smoking hams, bacon, and any meats in need of preserving by slow hickory smoking and salting down."

I can imagine the fragrance that wafted through Taylor Valley, mingling with neighboring smokehouses, to lay a blanket of aroma associated with "autumns of old" and a simpler time! By the time I experienced stays in the country, the little building was no longer used for its original task, yet she always kept her given name, "the smokehouse." She merely switched to other duties on the farm.

As a little kid, to me, she was merely an extension of the house. Even then, the boards were weathered, multi-shades of gray, and the slope roof leaked! This little squatty structure lived a higher degree of use in decades past—two rooms accommodating the tool shed/work area, all implements associated with country life!

To young Joy, it held areas of great interest—the box of copper nails, the mounted vise, wonderful and secretive boxes, dusty dirty. Yet there were hints of "what could be in here" to a curious little girl. I especially enjoyed it when Luke, Minnie, Patty, and myself would piddle in the smokehouse. Luke would create scraggly little copper rings by securing those nails in the vise, shaping, and pounding into a semblance of rustic jewelry. The smaller room held the corn bin and the crank style corn shucker, garden baskets, discarded potbelly stove, bedsteads, rolls of sisal rope, and garden stakes—a veritable smorgasbord of more "stuff" that piqued my curiosity!

A small wood plank porch stretched the entire length of the smokehouse with a narrow concrete walking path all the way to the back porch of the house. It was a dream for a little girl and her tricycle—the wooden porch served as both off ramp and turn about! It was through the eyes of a grandmother the day of "the old gals" (aka: smokehouse) photo session. I was thinking of angles, proper lighting, and such when I stepped back, really looking at it as more than a building.

It would be an injustice to describe such an aged structure as that of a graceful, stoic Victorian lady in the waning years of her wonderful southern style, bowing but graceful, accepting her imminent demise. As I had said, even at her inception, this was no beautiful structure, but serviceable and still utilized 70+ years later.

In the moment of maneuvering for the best photo, I did indeed think of her as a "wonderful old lady"—still squatty, still stout, as middle-aged ladies often get, grayer for certain, wearing her rusty disheveled roof, the wonderful wood plank porch disintegrated with time, somewhat leaning forward with warped time worn walls—a very humble, unassuming matriarch, and indeed a piece of Smith history! I sensed the old gal expressed an aura of finality for her life, the winter surroundings so appropriate, almost whispering her own epitaph.

The bittersweet experience of capturing the "smokehouse" took a reinforced spirit in the novice realm of my photographing abilities. It was as though this proud, stooped old structure assumed her own air of dignity, for the photos were certainly expressive and impressive.

Perhaps the outcome depicted the very soul of this matriarch. I like to think her eulogy was kind and appreciative and that the family will see her through the eyes of a little girl! This proud old lady stood with dignity, served with dedication and certainly worthy to grace our family SMITHSONIAN museum of memories.

Her photos shall be a lasting monument, and just as I am saddened by her empty rooms and tattered exterior, it's as though she waits until someone voices, "It's okay. Go peacefully—your duty is done." And I did.

The Seat of History

The seat I speak of isn't in our political backbone of D.C. or in Philadelphia, rich in history. It's not even in the Smithsonian, although this "seat" does qualify as a relic of the "Smith-Smithsonian."

This historical li'l seat sits stoically in an environment complimenting the rich history it represents, companied by other furnishings that have marched through time as "good friends."

There is nothing breathtaking or unique in design about the li'l highchair. It has always been present in the household, sort of taken for granted, changing colors through the years, changing occupancy even more so! There are no safety features, no attached tray, nothing that actually would be considered conducive for effectiveness in baby servitude! I do know the safety feature for security consisted of a diaper tying child to chair—the organization for child safety's worst nightmare!

With a century of service, the li'l chair sports worn rungs molded to the feet of many! I guess it's the equivalent of wrinkles on the weatherworn, aged faces of the children fortunate enough to experience the chair.

This small paragraph in our family history speaks loudly with its very unassuming presence, indicative of what I like to think expresses certain family qualities—basic design, not aesthetic, certainly not "Ethan Allen," but neither are the many li'l rear ends served by this chair. Somewhat roughhewn, yet smoothed and mellowed by time, just as life does to us all!

When there was a "rite of passage"—this being you outgrew the under-scale size seat, or just replaced by an up-and-coming babe—it wasn't open for debate. This fixture belonged to no individual and was never out of service in the household! So, the highchair of "quiet resolve" was always present! Easy to take for granted.

I wonder how many of us adults have sat in the chair—you know, during those weight loss times in our life. How many sat there in heartbreak, fear, dismay, or merely in quiet resolve? I think we all have a story that relates to the chair, and if the chair could regale tales, the volumes would fill a room!

Yes, the famous highchair has served the best and worst when it comes to "rear ends." The seat has been replaced several times, yet the signs of time are prominently displayed in the stately, proud, little unassuming highchair, still in service, standing quietly among old furniture it has diligently befriended through the years.

I think the terms "antique, classic, or vintage" would be an insult to the highchair. Truly, we should consider this rough little chair a diligent, familiar ole friend—ready to serve and seat!

I Gave the Best of What I Never Had

I knew my life had changed after the loss of my granddaddy, Bowers. He truly loved Jimmy and me. Little children just have that innate sense of knowing!

At the age of five, a whirlwind hit my young world. Daddy took Jim and I to a place that seemed so far removed and put us in the care of people we didn't know.

I guess that was the age my true strength and sense of survival grew and certainly was nurtured by the existing conditions and the "relatives" I hardly knew in the "country."

Looking back, I'm sure our aunt Jady was the primary caregiver. She was a young "spinster" sister of our Daddy. Although Gramps and Grandma Smith were also present in the clapboard house, I most definitely sensed that Jim and I were obligations, not welcomed grandchildren. Aunt Jady left no doubt that she had no love for us!

Now, most five-year-olds these days have fine clothes, food to eat, and the security of a home. I, as a five-year-old, often had to "find" clothes, am thankful for grease gravy and bread, and are aware that home was just a word in my world!

It was only when I became gravely ill while in "the country" that Daddy took me back to town to live with he and Ginny, my stepmother.

It was a degree of illness that no one expected me to live! Fast forward to 1943. I was in survival mode and had developed an "old soul," I guess. Ginny was expecting her first baby, and this 7-year-old was over the top excited! I didn't even want to go to school for fear of missing out on "the baby."

I think that it was during this wait that I vowed, "I'm going to love that baby, and it's going to love me."

On October 30, 1943, I arrived at the house after school to find a live baby doll! Mary Ellen had the roundest little face! A wisp of hair, big blue eyes so like a kewpie doll. I was breathless!

My vow to love this little baby girl came so naturally, and my plan was to take charge of her and care thereof!

It was probably less than a month that aside from feedings, baby Mary Ellen was in my charge, and this 7-year-old could never be happier.

There were diapers to change and soak. Keep in mind that this was the era of cloth diapers and no rubber pants, baths for the baby, which I gladly did, and those really special times that I snuggled her up close to me in my bed, kissed her little head, hummed a little song sometimes, and listen to her soft baby breathing as she went off to sleep, content to be in my arms.

That nurturing quality has been a mainstay all my life, through many more babies—both mine and those of others.

I'll end this little story by repeating, "I gave the best of what I never had," and baby Mary Ellen gave that love right back to me!

Honoring my sister, Barb, and Mary Ellen

Her Memory Vault

I always think of Barb more so this time of year, a time when she goes into her personal memory vault and removes the double locked box of love, memories, and loss.

Barb has a strong need to always stroll down her personal library of life and events. Some contents have "jagged edges and scars" that have left deep crevices and scars on her soul, yet with bittersweet resolve, she reaches into her vault pulls forward the "sonnet of her heart" to regale and to remember that which she would never have forgotten, even had she not done so.

Without a doubt, this is a sonnet of the truest love story I have ever been privileged to observe, sometimes with laughter, sometimes with just a headshake. By no means was Barb and Jay (aka: Paw Boy) sugar and spice all those years! It was the intertwined understanding that was something to behold! Paw Boy was a man of few (very few) words, yet his presence certainly deemed respect, and when he did indeed offer an opinion, it was worth the listen. Barb, well I have to be inclusive of myself and state that "we aren't without boisterous opinions" and strong feelings of what we deem "fair and just" or just manage to throw up a hand it the air, and with a glance "stop the show." I have watched Paw Boy's face offer up a crooked grin while Barb would be in the middle of a tangent over some injustice, or just shake his head with amusement. I can't ever recall being around when he disputed her opinion, and I don't think I would have wanted to be!

He loved as it should be, unconditional! He adored her and cared for her in ways women would envy, yet theirs was a private, understood communication that others could never be part of.

I know Barb walks the same rooms, yet it is not as it was. I know her heart sighs as she listens to the silent music of a soul in thought of her Paw Boy and the deafening silence as she speaks his name or listens to her heart's sweetest song that tell her the saddest thoughts. I also know there has to be "remembrances" that make her chuckle and wonder, "What was he thinking?" or, *what was I thinking?*

I know there have been times that tears would fall from her eyes and stay on her soul no one could comfort. I know there have been many times she cringed at going into her comfortable beautiful home, because half her soul was gone. I know there have been trips through her familiar surroundings just touching, smelling, looking, sitting, standing—a feeling of being lost and without cause for being.

Time eases grief, but not loss. It is her strength and caring for everyone that makes her an amazing woman!

I know that her soul still has those secret hours when the floodgate opens, for tears are indeed the safety valve of our hearts.

I also know that she has made so many happy times in my life that I could never forget, how glad that we have intersected during "times of our lives" and how proud I am of her tenacity and compassion, equally proud to call her my sister. I love you, Barb.

He's Had His Moments

I doubt that my brother, Luke, has a current library card, but the wisdom he maintains and imparts is a trait to be envied by any PhD in many fields of study!

He is a seeker of solitude on many levels. The physical solitude is misunderstood; his chameleon personality always allows others to *underestimate* him! His mental solitude is a vast personal vault that I'm not sure I could take a stroll through! Such a kaleidoscope labyrinth of private thoughts and life memories. It would be a humbling experience.

Luke maintains his exterior office within an arm's reach of his front door. His very presence exudes an aura of *"position and authority."* It is apparent by the placement of several chairs and other creature comforts surrounding this small perimeter of "Lukedom" that he is honored and sought out by many. He truly has his moments.

It is humorous to observe folks coming and going, acknowledging "Mr. Luke" in several forms of greetings—more humorous to hear his pure Southernese drawl emitting *an inaudible acknowledgement:* THEY UNDERSTAND! This is an awesome display of his Chameleon trait, being that he is a "well-spoken" man in total command of the Queen's English, *as well as a couple of other languages!* Diversity is his forte!

Thinking of Mr. Luke, I had one of those epiphanies that brought about my own *moment* of "I wonder."

I wonder if anyone has ever asked Mr. Luke, "What do you have to think about so much?" or, "Ever think you're wasting minutes just thinking so much?" or, "Aren't you bored? Go enjoy some life." *It would be a few seconds of suspended time awaiting his answer.*

Would Luke scratch his left ear, cross his arms, cock his head, look over his glasses and share his thinking about life as "a man child" growing up on Columbia Ave.? About *wasting time* hauling coal in the house when the bucket outweighed him? About moments of *enjoying* an Indian cigar? About worry and concern for three sisters?

Would he share little enjoyments of monopoly, mustard and onion sandwiches, and honey buns from the hog bread bags? Would he regale his *wasting time* running a mile or so from school on a 30-minute lunch to carry in wood/coal because it was going to rain?

Going forward in this chronological multiple choice of Luke's possible reply, would he maybe share the little *moments of enjoyment at foreign ports*, such as Spain, Greece, or other beautiful, mysterious places? Would he share *wasted time* spent in a far-off jungle with exotic names such as *Dogpatch (hill 327), Quang Tri, Da Nang, or Marble Mt.?*

Would he share his *boredom* experienced during the theatre performance of *The Tet Offensive*? Would he re-enforce that *wasted time* proudly and honorably serving in the Marine Corps? In that suspended time before reply, would Luke consider the *wasted moments* serving as a police officer? The *enjoyment* of temporary true love, the all-encompassing love of *the first born*, or the all-consuming "*Souler Eclipse*" at the loss of that child? In that moment, would he allow himself to reply with a mere *heart sigh*?

Would Luke share his *thinking* process at other successes and failures in life? Would he share the *boredom* of his living that most of us can only experience in movies or a good book? Would he reply at his *wasting time* teaching his young son to fry and flip eggs?

Would he perhaps impart wisdom of *personal hope* continuing his trek of thinking and wasting time *teaching his son to be a good and godly man?* He may reply in a manner reserved for someone like myself, someone he knows *he can be sure of*. He may reply with one of those famous Smith-style verbal tongue spankings.

Mr. Luke would most likely reply in his quaint southern drawl, "*Ya know, guess I've had my moments!*"

A Personal Christmas "Carol"

Here it is, Christmas 2002! It seems that Brad and Hannah decided on my gift months ago! A new baby! I had to admire the creative "hit and run" method in which the initial announcement of this new addition came. I received a greeting card with an additional little message: "#4 grandbaby! See you about December 25th!" Of course, Brad and Hannah were in the Bahamas when I received the card, thus the "hit and run" comment. Guess they wanted me to absorb that news before their return!

I am going to jump ahead to the present. Keith and I arranged with Brad, Hannah, and Michelle to meet in Jacksonville on Friday, Dec. 20, to have a family meal and visit with them. Elizabeth, Jessica, and Matthew rarely see each other, as working schedules and distance seems to deter regular visits.

We had a very pleasant gathering, of course talking of the expected "new addition" and Santa's* pending visit! Keith and I returned to South Carolina late into the night. I was pleased to know Michelle and Matthew were going to spend the night at Brads!

Since the weekend of the 22nd was quiet with no indication of "baby girl" joining us for Christmas, we went about normal business such as one would. We went to the grocery store Tuesday, picking up a few necessaries and delivering a gift. My request of Keith to stop by the "corner" on the way home was a common request. Let me explain "the corner."

About two years ago, a corner at the church was designated as a memorial to all unborn babies—those aborted children. I have always taken that little memorial quite personal and have insured fresh flowers were always present.

This act has never been for recognition. For the most part, Keith has been the only person familiar with my dedication to this. Well, as usual, I knelt to whisper my own little prayer, including as always the kids, grandkids, and the health of little Carol. I replaced the mums with the poinsettia, and as I stood, my legs felt like putty. I attributed this to my quick ascend up and fluctuation of my blood pressure. Normal. As I jumped back into the truck to ride the couple of blocks back to our house, it felt as though warm water was poured inside of me! That's the only way to describe this!

Starting at my head down to my feet—and I verbally gave a little "phew-w-w." We came into the house, bringing in parcels. The temporary experience was put aside, and I went to the sink to run some water. The fragrance that wafted from my hands was overpowering as I put both hands up to my nose, exclaiming to Keith, "Smell this!" Fresh, sweet, strong! It was a cross between roses and baby powder. The warmest sensation hit me directly in my upper torso.

The phone rang. Keith answered to Brad informing us that "little Karol" was on her way. I knew before the phone was handed to me. It was as though the very essence of all those little ones never to be, those babies I pray for and care for, were in mass chiming out, singing to my very soul and assuring me without words that all would be fine. Little Karol was to make flight from heaven with cheers from the little ones that did not complete their journey. This was a day and event she needs to know of! What a gift she gave me before her arrival.

Little Renee "Karol" Fleenor made her entrance the following morning, Dec. 24 at 8:08 a.m. Thanks, baby girl!

She is Our Sunshine

Often, I look at a picture and truly see symbolism at its best. This was the case as I admired a picture taken of Barb standing in a field of sunflowers. How appropriate that her choice of wardrobe complimented the flowers. We who know Barb best are aware of her hierarchy within the family tapestry. That she is the one who can shoulder the weight of any problem or situation we selfishly present her with and somehow present resolve!

This isn't a skill or recognition that comes with age! Oh, no. I can personally recall dilemmas from an early age where I just knew that because Barb was there, it would be handled! This could simply be needing syrup put in my bottle (yes, I shamelessly admit sucking one till about the age of five) or feet washed. She always had a little extra money to pay my way for movies or the skating ring.

As I grew into adulthood, so did the dilemmas, and I always called on Barb first for guidance and advice. It was selfish of me, as I look back.

The one fact I do know is that I wasn't alone looking to Barb for comfort and resolve, and for that I still feel selfish for not only myself but for all the others! Now, allow me to share what I see in the marvelous picture. I see Barb observing all those friends, family members, and often those she crossed paths with once or twice.

I see "all of we sunflowers" looking in one direction, toward Barb!

I see Barb admiring the growth and strength of all her "flowers" she has guided and advised, and in the forefront I see the forlorn saddened "flowers" yet to be brought about in strength and hope by the very crossing life intersections with Barb.

I don't think Barb knows the impact of her love and guidance to we "flowers" in her life! But she should know the love and lineage as we "flowers" continue to stand tall and look to her as sunshine in so many lives.

I love you Barb. You have been there to dust my knees off and make me stand taller.

Barb passed away on December 18, 2019, at age 82. I was honored to be with her several weeks before and when she passed away. Miss you, sister.

Heavenly Sunshine

On July 13, 2000, the White/Wright family reunion took place at the home of my cousin, David Shumaker, and his gracious wife, Annie. This was the perfect home for such an event. It stands proudly and stoically at the corner of Holston Ave. in Bristol, Tennessee, quiet witness to many generations of families—those who have lived within its walls, hugged by the rich wood, and the vintage furnishings. It was obvious this home had been nurtured and appreciated, also graced with a backyard conducive for any large group such as this clan event!

It was easy to parallel this home's qualities to that of the family celebrating the reconnection of my mama's siblings, cousins, and friends, as well as the generations cascading down that family tree just as a small brook would roll on consistent in its flow—with occasional spurts of quickened waters. Such as in all families, there was the occasional "spurt" of births adding to the "family membership," those additions which also cascade and develop into a new, fragile little branch on their birthright tree.

Nancy Privett, Mama's baby sister, spearheaded this event with the precision and regimentation of a salty old military general, and did so from long distance. I'm not exactly sure who served as "Bristol Connection" for this strategical event, but my educated guess, based on the "to do" list, is that Mary Ellen (Minnie) carried a major share of this well-orchestrated get together as well as other local family members. Indeed, it took a successful team effort to "make it happen" as folks meandered onto the grounds. I couldn't deny my inquisitive nature as I put names, places, and events certain family members had impressed on me as I grew up—some indelible characters to say the least! A kaleidoscope collage of those sharing the common threads of family. I guess similar to a woven tapestry, family "threads" can also separate, wear thin, and leave behind sections that look "thread barren." Even when a tapestry suffers this obvious violation, the worn area is most likely to be strategically covered by a piece of furniture, just as family clans too often choose covering up such "flaws" or ignoring the obvious indicators that scream out something not so positive is taking place within a branch of my family. I remind myself how remiss I have been and that I will probably continue to be less than perfect. Such is my tapestry—serviceable, but nonetheless flawed.

This collective gathering of Whites, Wrights, and ex in-laws once active members of my family welcome just the same—several friends and old neighbors merely catching up with family additions and news, and as conversation continued, I noticed the hub of each story seemed to be my mama, Virginia (White) Smith. After all, she was the oldest of nine. Losing her mother in her teenage years, she became the caretaker of her younger siblings, and as I found out later by reading vintage letters from her "elders" (1937), she tenaciously stood her ground to keep the family together, not allowing "relatives with good intentions" to relieve her young shoulders of this responsibility.

The previous reunion was 1996, same locale. This celebration was also without the presence of Mama, her brother, Jessie, or Daddy. No one expected the loss of "the elite inspiration," Robin (Smith) Brooke, the strongest, delicate young lady, reveling in her role as wife and mother. If I listen close, the unique laughter of Robin resounds and lifts my spirit, just as she did and continues to do so in many lives. She knew sadness, yet never put it out for others to see. Robin's passing proves that "God often takes the prettiest and best flowers in his garden."

Robin's absence at the 2000 reunion was such a rip on our family tapestry, and her beautiful daughter, Summer, reflected her mom's attributes. I saw a young widower, suffering silently through this reminder of his loss. I observed a mother/grandmother, Wanda, being outwardly jovial while carrying tears on her soul that never will go away. I observed a father (Luke) displaying this same "starch," yet when there was occasion for Luke and Wanda to make eye contact, the degree of grief and loss was equal. Luke not only lost a child, but also he lost his best friend, confidant, and one-woman cheerleader to her dad.

Again, we did not expect the 2000 reunion to be the last for Uncle Charles, and we don't know what the next gathering will bring. Personally, my mind was in a fog in 1996 on divorce overload. So, I was pretty much wrapped up in me. This makes for a "pretty small package." At the 2000 reunion, I had a renewed soul, clarity of mind, and I was happy in my life, with Keith and I celebrating three years of marriage already. I was content as his wife, and we were (and still are) kindred spirits!

Perhaps my deepened appreciation for family brought about my overwhelming thoughts, although no person with a conscience validates the loss of their parent(s). My 15-year attitude of "unfair loss" of Mama was softened. The grudge I had been carrying vaporized. How selfish I was! How could I wish mama still here? There was no doubt she was in paradise. Why would I want to see her suffer over losing Jessie and Charles? Above all, why would I want to see her at the graveside of her beautiful granddaughter and observe her grandsons, now grown men, shattered and broken as they tenderly moved Robin's casket? Why in the world would I want to see Mama perhaps totally spiritually broken? No doubt Mama was there, arms outstretched, as Robin and her contagious laugh entered the heavenly kingdom. Most likely, Mama was singing "You Are My Sunshine," as she had sung to all her grandchildren at one time or another. Mama and the kids had a unique "mutual admiration society." She left sweet memories and happiness come through doors she didn't even know she left open! All the grandchildren were teens when they lost the most special granny. Their grief ran so deep, and although Mama and Daddy were not physically here when little Luke was born, surely they peep in once in a while to gloat over their youngest grandson!

The organized chaos and escalating conversations among so many intertwined with common threads, literally diminished to my sense of hearing. I was studying the immense display of pictures and information on family members past and present, and whether my imagination was kicking into gear or it was a heaven-sent gift, soft whispers and the muted chortled laugh Mama often spewed out was in my ears! I looked around to see if there was reaction from others milling around, which there wasn't, but I became aware that I was humming "You Are My Sunshine, My Only Sunshine," bringing a comfort and unconscious smile! It's one of those times you have to look to the heavens and whisper, "Thanks."

The very spirit and bonds of love punched through to oversee the family—the teenage grandchildren, now adults with children of their own, Mama and Daddy's "kids," now grannies and granddaddies! As I settled into a spot of advantage, watching the professional photographer attempting to get the little ones to settle down ("great grands" to Mama and Daddy), it was similar to stacking B.B.'s—both futile efforts!

Taking advantage of the few little ones who were actually sitting still, or at least leaving at a slow trot, I managed to snap three pictures with the old 35 mm camera. It was necessary to take all from the same angle in order to be quicker than their attention span and fast little feet. I had no idea if any of these three pictures would develop into more than a blur. I saw at least a few others struggling for that same shot. I wonder if success was theirs? I can still picture this visual of the kids—an exasperated photographer spilled over as Mary Ellen, Luke, Patty, and I posed for a generational picture. I had an obvious "perm grin," totally recalling the scene with the kids and distraught photographer.

The finished photos were ready to pick up before I left Bristol coming back to South Carolina. The picture of the four of us was okay. The angle was such that it appeared we were all looking up, and the stream of sun enhanced the background. The real gift depicting that day of reunion came later when I picked up the several rolls of developed film! I had handed my camera to one of the family teenagers, requesting he take a picture of the four Smith kids while we posed for the photographer. Apparently, the 10-second lesson I had given on camera workings failed! Yet, amazingly, the sunbeam had radiated in translucent yellow as though to bath us in "heavenly sunshine."

This Sunday school song of my childhood popped into my head! Regardless of any opinions, I am confident this was a special gift from the very heavens. Perhaps our heavenly father allowed Mama, Daddy, Robin, and others unknown to us to open that spiritual portal, spilling out the gift of heavenly sunshine.

When I came to the photographs which delighted me so, some were of the great grandchildren—the first two being about what I expected! Will Bowers was walking away, the others chatting among themselves, oblivious to the frustrated photographer. And seated to the far right was Vicki White's daughter and Charles and Hallie's granddaughter. Oh well—kids are kids!

The prints were clear but not frameable. When I came to the third, the picture, position, and pose took my breath away! I literally laid it down on my kitchen bar, observed it from a distance, placed the other two beside of it for comparison, and for no conscience reason felt tears welling up in my eyes.

Granted, I have had experiences—miracles, if you will—but this wonderful, timeless picture was indeed the finest gift. The beams of rainbow colors and sunlight washed over these babies! Talk about a heavenly gift. Strangely enough, the beams went behind Vicki's daughter. It doesn't matter what others see; I know it was a display of acknowledgment from the very heavens, and Mama would indeed do such an act!

This was the only time I set out to disprove my theory. I asked the professionals in this field because sun and lens can make strange optical effects. The bottom line to what happened is, "I don't have any idea."

The negative was the same, the other two shots are identical. We discussed refracted angles, slopes, etc. The result of this particular picture had no rhyme or reason, no explanation of physics in photography, no special lens, and no intricate extension lens. So, I share this with anyone willing to believe!

I proudly have the print framed, entitled "Heavenly Sunshine," although in the old hymnal, the song is titled "Heavenly Sunlight." That's okay. After all, a rose is a rose. A miracle is, well…A miracle is a wonderful gift to cherish.

Nature's Art Museum

The ability to paint has long been a desire at the very core of my soul! The artwork in my mind is breathtaking, yet the ability to transfer that majestic illustration eludes me. The admiration I have for those talented people with that innate natural ability borders on coveting!

Sure, I expound with glee when I manage to stay in the lines of any coloring book.

In the early spring of 2002, when I was marveling at the hues of the flowers and foliage, I had a memory from a cobwebbed section of my brain, the section reserved for "innocence of youth."

I recalled the very first garment I sold and how it was embellished for appeal. The little handstitched semblance of a doll dress, made from a scrap of white sheet. Even at this early age, I really think I had a grasp on marketing a product, and strangely enough, 43 years later, the same process influenced "color by nature."

The little dress was natural deco. I placed it on the floor of my playhouse, commenced placing little yellow buttercup flowers facedown, then whacked each flower with a rock at the neck and skirt bottom. Then, I displayed beautiful yellow borders! Compliments of nature, and I was 25 cents richer thanks to Janice Paige!

Back to the current century, I said to myself, "Self", merely because I always listen to the voices. I am pursuing the process again, with more sophisticated tools and better hand-eye coordination.

I had duck cloth to use as my canvas and acquired pansies from the hospital landscape. I somewhat think of it as a contribution to fine arts, and it eases my guilt inverting the first pansy on the cloth. I put into play my sophisticated tool: a big hammer. Keith, too, joined me in this style of real art! Think about this. We never had color mix problems and needed an "eye for art" as to shading and shadows. And we had managed to capture reflections of a season to enjoy and share with others! I was so impressed that Mary Ellen had the one canvas made for her framed and displayed! I guess I expected it to rank up there with other Frigidaire art.

You could say the beautiful bounty of "nature's art" cannot be embellished or improved. I'm just thankful for buttercups of long ago and the influence of my "inner child" shelved away in the library of my mind!

Ed's Elfin Era

Eddie Joe Bowers has the distinct position of seeing the entire Smith family through the eyes of a lovestruck, old-soul teenager, so he has indeed the seniority of "long term" involvement. Thank God! He and Minnie have shared 40 years together, and since I am falling through the portal of "fivey-two" (doesn't that sound much better than fifty-two?), I qualify to also mirror back my observations!

Wishing to be as complimentary as possible, Ed was a family man. ALWAYS THERE. He was successful in his "serious career," always constant in his priority of "encapsulated family." Also, Eddie was AWARE. He was an observer, more so than a participant, when it concerned matters outside his home! Be advised! As aloof as his personality emitted, his tenacity to provide for and protect his wife (my sister) and his sons, Brit and Brian, would be similar to that of a pit bull! I don't think that was ever proven; I don't feel anyone would question or challenge him!

Although there wasn't a lot of interaction with the Bowers family within my chapters of life, we had "normal"–family Christmases at Mama's, passing in visits, keeping up through messages, etc. At some point, Eddie Joe became "Ed." I respect that, but he will always be Eddie Joe to me, just as Mary Ellen is Minnie!

If this story seems to ramble, singing the praises of a "long term" brother-in-law, know it is absolutely necessary in order for someone outside "those in the know" to get the impact of how out of character this accidental talent was.

Eddie Joe was the Ozzie to our Minnie's Harriet, the Ward Cleaver to Minnie's role of June. Typical businessman, long-term planner, wrapped in the comfort of home, family, and his God. There are no illusions that family differences within their realm failed to exist! Or no illusions that the rose garden of fairytale marriage was without thorns! Yet their strife in life, like their love, was very personal. Ed's success reflects through two fine grown men, and Ed slipped into the role of granddaddy quite naturally.

Let's get to the subject the chapter title states! Eddie's Elfin Era began with the gift of a woodcarving set about three years ago. Well, Grandaddy Ed could have "whittled" such items of older appreciation, like designer toothpicks or perhaps graduated to flutes, or like myself, simply put the carving set on a shelf! It's always amazing how people are instrumental in "life choices!" The Ed I know pretty much served as the "inspiration" or the "fan" to anyone seeking to aspire. I truly believe there are no coincidences, and the visit with his "whittlin'" friend, Harold, was no exception.

I'm gonna fast forward here ... Ed's ability and the art he produces is truly amazing! In order to make clear exactly how much of a pleasant surprise this was, and for the sake of impact and understanding, let's compare this. It would be like if the Russian Ballet featured me (merely by a phone call), or if someone in our family received the Nobel Peace Prize (for no reason). Or if Luke was auspiciously placed in the baseball hall of fame! Okay, I think the point is made. When Keith and I visited, and the initial "first" carvings were presented—the ax in the chopping block, the initial 3-inch teardrop Santa ornaments, one or two little square torso, simple Santas. Speechless IS the word! Ole unassuming Ed took the compliments in simple stride. To this day, I still think he doesn't recognize what an ARTIST and CRAFTSMAN he truly is! If that capability was "the music in my soul" as it is to Ed, I wouldn't be able to ask for more.

In such a very short time, he has expanded his line of carvings and taken up more garage space! He even "allowed" Minnie to participate—painting, embellishing, transporting, accounting. In other words, she was his Chief Elf in R&D!

Now, it may be because it was a time in his life, about half past "common sense" age, that this talent reared its head. Or it is a suppressed talent that has been steeping within his soul for years. Regardless, Ed is certainly leaving a tangible epitaph—a happy monument, so to speak, as he acknowledges the fun of his creations, and in the true spirit of Eddie Joe, a fair financial gain. KEEP A-WHITTLIN', ED! You just stay humble; I'll express the delight for you! With pride (and still surprise), Joy is your #1 fan.

King Memorial Church

Mama saw to it that we had spiritual growth and guidance. We were fixtures at the little church on Heather Rd. King Memorial was a small wood frame structure, although it is now bricked. The sight of this "staple of my kidhood" whisked up memories of so long ago—sounds of sermons, kids laughing, Ed Feathers' deep harmony reverbing, the commanding voice of Paul Nelson, and those gone on except in my "Hall of Wisdom" memory.

We four Smith kids walked to Sunday school approximately 5-6 blocks. It seemed a longer distance to my shorter legs! On Sunday nights, Daddy drove Mama and we "youngins" to services. I recall Mama's credo was to say to us, "Do you know what makes little girls pretty? To act pretty."

I don't recall Luke being kept in check with words of wisdom, probably because he was outside smoking one of his Indian cigars prior to leaving for Sunday school. We all had "good" clothes on, complete with white gloves that also served as "coin holder" for my offering money so that it would stay secure. There was one occasion I failed to put my offering into Sunday school plate, and the rest of my day was ruined by fear of some personal cataclysmic heavenly punishment.

We were always receiving "attendance honors" for vacation bible school and Sunday school. The attendance of familiars was an understood, and for the most part, everyone claimed the same pews! The "elders" of the church, such as Miss Mac and Dr. Ebersole, deemed a higher respect from a younger Joy. "Intimidating" is the appropriate term. The other families, such as The Worlies, Kessees, Ketrons, Caulfields, Snotgrasses, Feathers, Testers, Rileys, Nelsons, Gentrys, and others that came passing through, summed up to about 70-85 folks total! I'm sure our little church could never accommodate 150 people.

This was an innocent time, the '50s, and it was acceptable to allow children's Halloween parties, Easter egg hunts, and Christmas parties to be celebrated with pomp and pageantry. In 1957, due to the measles, I missed attending the class Christmas party, but Mrs. Tester and Nora Riley sent me a shoebox full of cookies, Cheetos, a soggy sandwich, and an apple as well as a little party favor. In 1959, I received the grand prize for finding the special Easter egg, located under the front cinder block step at the road.

In 1962, Mary Ellen and Eddie Joe were married in our little church on Heather Rd., and as a little sister, I felt very special.

It's Just a Doll

Have you ever been skimming through the memory bank of your kidhood and come to a screeching halt at your tiny little brain shelf, dusty and cobwebbed, that wonderful place where you have stored away all those dolls you enjoyed? Take a few minutes to wipe off that "smudged" window, blow away some dust, visit some of old companions, and bestow on them a little hug just as you used to.

A few years ago, my oldest sister Mary Ellen (aka: Minnie) innocently inspired me to consider the value of receiving such a cherished prize without realizing the true gift was "the very act of giving." Mary Ellen is by nature a "giver" with an ability to match a gift to the recipient, so what would prompt her to bestow a doll upon our grown niece? Minnie should know that, by sharing this story, the gift became mine to ponder, appreciate, and pass on.

I vividly recall each and every doll I ever received! At age 5, I was devastated when I became Mama to a redhead with plastic ponytail. Guess this was the ultimate "red headed step-child." My favorites were the hard plastic "baby doll"—no hi-tech features such as those today. The most interesting one I parented had a tube from oral orifice directly to "where gravity took it." I remember putting Kool Aid, coffee, pancake syrup, and other semi-liquids down her chute.

On any given night, one or more shared the bed with me, but considering the rubber and plastic component of these effigies in conjunction with the below-freezing temperatures of our unheated upstairs rooms, well, I should have preferred furry stuffed animals such as Minnie and Patty. Most likely, they had a better understanding of basic warmth! This brings up another empty validation for one of my shortcomings and my sisters' strengths! My maternal skills were used up on inanimate dolls, whereas they had all that good Mothering reserved. I'll have to add that to my lame excuse list.

Dolls served as a training tool for motherhood, however the commonsense age of fivey-o is in my rear-view mirror, so knowledge is mine!

If you needed to have a little cry, couldn't you hug a baby doll and spill your "heart hurts" and tears, able to embellish whatever situation you sobbed out knowing she would keep the secret? Sing a less than perfect lullaby with silent appreciation? Share wishes, wants, and woes, embracing her with a secure hug when YOU were in need of one? JUST A DOLL!

Minnie, you always knew. Before child therapist, long before comatose-inducing control medications we give our children, we had our "silent sentries"—always with a smile, our dolls.

We grandmas are merely antique little girls! JUST A DOLL! Like the Grand Canyon is just a hole in the ground, the Moon is just a rock, and a Sister is just another person. Thanks, Minnie.

That Simple Life

It was during a conversation with Barb that she brought up her grandchildren cannot believe the lifestyle we lived growing up.

Now, Jim, Barb, and Bill Smith were the post-depression era, pre-WWII kids, whereas Mary Ellen and Luke were "in the midst of WWII" kids. Patty and I slid in as post-war, early baby boomers.

Barb was the primary onsite babysitter, housekeeper, and errand girl during the stint on Norfolk Ave., which was merely a suburb of the seedy Kingtown section of Bristol, Virginia. This "estate on the hill" lacked plumbing, thus the backyard sported a lovely clapboard toilet which I'm sure was a "one-seat facility." Being that there was no running water inside the house, it was necessary to heat hot water on the coal-burning cook stove. There are many "working parts" to this task—the coal had to be carried into the house, all ashes removed and dumped, then you'd grab up the kerosene can, hoping you had some. Otherwise, Barb's errand-running title came into play, and she'd trot to the store.

Wad up paper, throw in some kindling (sticks), light it up, toss in some coal, throw on some kerosene, and stand back! Regardless of the season, the cook stove stayed "fired up!" The other stove in living room was for heat only, however the process was the same.

With black coal comes black "pebbles" and black dust all over the floors, so I guess that sanctioned all smokers to "duck" their cigarettes on the floor. How does this sound to all you grands and great grands?

Keep in mind, this process was every day. Certainly no payment other than room and board. The term "room" is too generous! Barb shared a bed with all other youngins who were not sleeping in a baby bed. I'm sure there were many "warm and wet" ice cold mornings Barb woke up wondering if her life would ever get better, and probably wondering if there were any good size cigarette ducks on the living room floor she could enjoy!

The morning meal was, for the most part, cooked oatmeal (once the fire on the cook stove was hot enough), so there was a lot of time and strategy involved during this time of morning. The kids could be dressed in front of the oven door while the water started to boil. Shoes had to be located (since everyone had one pair each) and pull-out socks with the least holes in toes or heel.

Doing laundry wasn't "daily" as you know it; laundry was a planned "laundry day." The wringer washer had to be set up as well as the double rinse tubs. All water had to be heated on the cook stove, keeping in mind even in summer you had a fire going. The baby clothes were always done first (in clean water) then scaled down, load after load after load—you get the jest. And you prayed for a good line drying day outside, otherwise lines were strung throughout the interior of the house for drying purposes.

Canning food was another entertaining concept! As summer veggies and fruits came in, the canning commenced. Inclusive of Barb's regular daily duties, she had the skinny hand to reach inside the nasty spider nest and moldy glass jars to wash and sanitize them in scalding water. Not bad for a 10- to 14-year-old!

Barb also attended the "required-by-law" school during this barrage of the so-called "simple" life.

So, when Barb's grands and great grands are amazed at her tenacious spirit, hard work ethic, her uncanny ability to overcome obstacles and take on any "windmills" in life…Well, ya'll just try the same "simple life" to build those characteristics that never cease to amaze you.

HUMOROUS STORIES

Family Rumblings

Oh, to be a child held "not accountable" at family gatherings! Wasn't it simple when the only active part the youngins played was to "go play" and stay out of the line of fire? I yearn for the blissful ignorance and lack of vocabulary to even care when the adults were having a difference of opinion, often forgetting the rules of civility.

The #1 event for at least an annual "bashing" is Thanksgiving, however this becomes boring as we grow into adulthood and are forced to muddle our brains with other stuff! I personally think this internal family bashing should be refined, modified, and personalized. Since the burden of role model falls upon the shoulders of adults, we should strive to "get it right."

Keep in mind, some will revert back to indignation of past years vs. months! It seems that inclusion of the calendar year up to November is a successful time frame. Thus, it stifles escalation to the point of weaponry and medical assistance, not to mention how upset Mama gets when uninvited paramedics violate the family circle.

The time allowance per individual is tricky, so this is optional since we all have that ONE (or more) crazy, dramatic, whining relative who insists on center stage! This is the same one thriving on descriptions of her/his most current physical malady. Ever notice within that description the standard statement, "Worst doctor I've seen in 40 years"? Or "Doc said it's a miracle I made it this far"? Does that emit some truth for your family dynamics? Oh, by all means, assign an individual to keep an eye on the alcohol indulgent member! They tend to kind of "throw a stick in the spokes" if allowed to give their foggy opinion.

Well, it's tough to determine a specific guideline as to locale. Factors such as inclement weather, pecking order of son/daughter in-laws present, timing of the "baby crying the most" (short fuse on a Mom who just won't SHUT THAT YOUNGIN UP), that situation will guarantee a bedroom starting point. Lord forbid that the senior matriarch be menopausal! She can "clear a room" with a glance, not to mention "clear the table" with one swing of her arm. It's this malady which dictates and/or supersedes ALL RULES.

One also needs to acknowledge topics that should be "disallowed," i.e., gender identity crisis, sloven traits, weight problems (females only), promiscuity (male and female), or any one of 1,000 mental health issues! Within your family, you have the right (perhaps not the ability) to establish "no holds barred" ruling. Keep in mind, there will most likely be blood drawn early on, so you may want to eat first. Oh, the pleasure of "no accountability." Of course, you will then be labeled "the slow child" or "not quite right." Know what? That could be used to an advantage! Just mumble, drool, cross your eyes once in a while—that's a guarantee you will get your plate of food FIRST! You'll most likely be seated alone to enjoy a peaceful meal. That also gives latitude when you "slam" that cousin with the baseball bat or spew forth words that would shock any sailor. You get total control of the TV remote. Hey, you adults are great role models! Pass the medication and "bless this food and family."

Consumers Lose

DO I HAVE A NEWS FLASH! Have you noticed the conversion of weights and measures displayed prominently on the packages we purchase at any retail store? I don't remember voting for this UNIVERSAL change. Over the last decade, I have noticed the shaved ounces from soups, sugar, flour, even the holy grail of beverages like coffee. Manufacturers have insured the package or maintained the same size and added more colorful labels! That distracts us from the real issue of shrinkage.

The simplicity of proof is as follows. A common area for independent research is your supermarket of choice, although there will be a need for actually reading the label vs. grabbing the familiar package. Marketing departments rely on the fact we are an impatient, fast society, and PRETTY appeals to us.

If you are a little rusty on math, just remember that there are 8 ounces to a cup, then multiply that accordingly. No! You aren't imagining what you see on shredded cheese, proudly illustrating and numbering that their product is indeed 2 cups of product, although the total weight is 8 ounces. How about 6 ounces being 2 cups, or the fact that 11.5 or 13 ounces is now a pound? Has anyone alerted Betty Crocker, Martha Stewart, Emeril, or the Ragin Cajun? Oh, my goodness, I have passed on recipes that are blatantly bogus! How do I recant the shame I feel at obvious "lack of math skills?"

Has anyone made this public knowledge to our children struggling to put "weights and measures" in perspective? Parents, be advised, do not use product size as a teaching tool. This will produce a deep neurosis when your child is implicated in a SCAM of deceit within a structured classroom setting! Woe is the student of commercial fraud, even more WOE to the consumer accepting this fraud! So, have we become so financially fluent that this is trivial information? Do we continue to accept the equivalent of P.T. Barnum's "THIS WAY TO THE GREAT EGRESS?" I certainly feel violated and stupid. Pointing out this shaved weight to corporations (yes, I write letters), you get a wonderful flowery form letter with a free coupon on their product of your complaint, thus adding insult to injury.

The miniscule degree of personal satisfaction is to return the letter as Unsolicited, with their coupon marked "VOID." Yes, I realize this act is similar to "giving a whale a tic-tac," but so what? If I weren't so "marketing cynical," these manufacturers would be in charge of guaranteed personal weight loss programs. Maybe I'm onto something! Watch out, Jenny Craig and Weight Watchers! No effort weight loss. Wow.

Southernese Shortcuts or English Words & Phrases, Southern Style

We Southern folk, for the most part, are considered just a tad slow when it comes to verbalizing "The Queen's English." You must understand, however, this doesn't insult we "Yodas of Southernese." Make no mistake—slow speaking doesn't mean we are slow-witted. I think we of the southern region enjoy being underestimated, but when the boundaries of civility are crossed, we offer a few options of retaliation:

1. BE IGNORED.
2. GET A TOOTHLESS SMIRK FROM A SOUTHERN GENT.
3. GET YOUR OWN TEETH KNOCKED OUT BY A SOUTHERN LADY!

For the sake of clarity, before I enlighten you readers with our Southernese, be advised we DO INDEED have educational institutes that expand our knowledge past a 4th grade level. WE DON'T live in clapboard shacks, marry our cousins, shoot our supper, smile with two or three teeth visible, or upgrade toilet facilities by digging a new hole for the outhouse. We especially don't condone joking about our slow, drawn-out manner of speech! Our dialect is totally understood when conversing with others from the South, and we often have no need to complete a thought process by verbalizing. To really impress you, Southernese is actually classified as bilingual! If you are unsure of the use of Latin, French, or Greek integrated into Southernese, remember we take shortcuts with words and phrases. Enjoy these examples. This verbiage is born and bred south of the Mason Dixon line. Makes me proud, ya'll!

EXPEL – "My ex spells my name wrong on dem papers."
EFFACE – "Bubba got efface purty beat up."
EWER (Latin) – "Ewer or yer sister needs to help Pa."
HERMIT – "Hermit to, but forgot."
How about the simple word HERMIT – ("Hermit to, but forgot")?
Or GNAW – ("My answer to that is gnaw")?
GNOME – "Gnome, Ma'am."
EXPOUND – "My ex pounded da crap outta my girlfriend." (She probably knocked out some dem teeth of the girlfriend. See again #3 option.)
We all know the word ILLBRED – "How 'bout ill bread to go wif that soup?"
Exclusive big, old words are used too! IDIOSYNCRASY (Greek) – "My boy called Idiot since es crasy."
Or, flaunting nautical knowledge (unbeknownst), such as HAWSE – "Gonna ride my hawse to the garden."

Southernese also utilizes the animal kingdom in normal conversation.

Take the GNU (of antelope family) – "Bubba gnu he was in trouble."
More impressive Latin, GEOMETRID – "Gee, Ole Maw tried."
How about JURASSIC? – "Jer ass ic some kinda trouble, Bubba."
LAICIZE – "She be talking laicize she got no sense."

Or along the same lines, LACKADAISICAL - "Maw speak of kid experience lack a daisical that done gone by." (Look that word up, it's there.)

Let's go with HOWDAH - "How dah been doin, nabor?"

We folks of practicing Southernese have utilized high-tech entitlements now recognized by OTHERS wanting to show their smartness!

How about the term "Job Control Language?" Although this is the term for one computer communicating with other computers, we Southernese use this phrase (JCL) as, "The boss said so, or I'm fired."

How about the Bell Curve used in our educational grading system? Well, we use the term as a geographical directional! "If ya'll go on down the road a piece, there's an old Oak tree on the left as ya take a sharp right at Bell curve."

The Jordan Curve is used as a geometrical term, but we know that somewhere beyond (or before ya get to) the Bell curve is the Jordan place. Yep, on a curve!

As I look over this small example of Southernese, it's clear that any more at this point would be overwhelming! After all, you need to really PONDER the philosophy of our language. Perhaps I need to leave it here and letcha have summin' to look forward to—Chapter 2. See ya'll later.

It's Jest English

Have you ever just listened to the English we use in normal conversation? Once again, the plateau in my brain switched to the humor component, although that is a "happy place"—sort of the Fisher-Price, colorful, bold, easy to grasp gray matter. I sometimes feel such personal observations come a little too easy for me!

If you care to look through the opposite end of my binoculars for a while, join me as I share a comical view of language we use every day.

I pay homage to my #1 favorite word, THWART. It seems to imply a speech impediment, possibly a lost abbreviation for "the wart!" Same goes for CAULKING. It just seems like a mispronounced word. Or how about TITHE? In no way do I imply disrespect to the meaning of tithing, yet doesn't that just bring out a vision of doing laundry, or a rhyming phrase of Tai-chi?

There are just so many comical components when I think of our English, most of which we adopted from Latin, Greek, or my favorite source, UNKNOWN. We have certainly been and continue to be guilty of shredding the Queen's English! After all, a queen can't possibly be "word usage cop," so we skip merrily along, dispronouncing* our English of mutilation.

When it comes to learning English of Choice, how can a child not be confused? We pronounce letter perfect words, with many multiple meanings and definitions! Consider the word "angle." This is one I always misspelled—still do! And to add to the confusion, this word has 13 definitions in the New Webster's dictionary. How about normal everyday words such as pen/pin, mall/maul, mail/male, chic/sheik—you get the jest of this maze of uncorrect* English we force our kids to learn, right? Or write/rite! We refined English speaking citizens also acquired words from Scandinavia, Norwegians, and certainly didn't leave out the Chinese.

We should have DO OVERS and create a simple, user-friendly language. I suggest "SOUTHERNESE." After all, it's friendly, versatile, colorful, and the use of incomplete sentences is a given and totally understood amongst us when speaking to each other. Another confusing segment to phrase usage is the word "OXYMORON." I remember how comical this was to me when I first heard it. It reminded me of "Babe the Blue Ox" of Paul Bunyan (or bunion) fame. Why do those powerful, educated folks feel at ease using such words as OMBUDSMAN (should be "I'm a Bud man"). If you spoke Southernese, that phrase is understandable! (Yes, I know it should be "an understood.")

Or how about EMULSION? Close to Creomulsion huh? What exactly warrants use of MOGUL? If that was Southernese, it would be a furren (not foreign) car! I choose (or chews) to poke fun at a few other words too (or "to" or "two"). How about ODIOUS or OBEY? Say those out loud to yourself. Now, doesn't that put a new twist to ridiculous sounding? How about the word STATISTICS? I think my daddy was the king of Southernese without realizing it!

I understand sa-stik-ticks (as he pronounced it), or ka-stroph-ta-sea (catastrophe). My goodness, Daddy could be king of the Nubba-Sudan Tribe, the seat of all language! It is now up to us to preserve his Avant Garde use of the Southernese form of English. Couldn't forget the French! Another observation on a particular word of violation: if an Islet (or eyelet) is merely a small Isle, then is a noselet a smaller nose? This is where one would assume (a word that makes an ASS of U and ME) I am an ole country bumpkin. Well, I am! At least the title of bumpkin made the Dictionary. Of course, Priggish and Persnickety and Riff Raff also qualify, just as anal-retentive earned paper space in the ole Webster's. I think there's some current words I'll keep in my quest for Southernese acceptance.

Keep in mind, "RIGHT OF ASYLUM" IS NOT (KNOT) ALWAYS (ALL WAYS) A FOREIGN EMBASSY!

If you wonder where that last statement fit into the summation, it doesn't! But I sure enjoy stating it!

* *My own recreated words.*

Acts of Compassion & Humanity or Felony or Misdemeanor

Anonymity has been mine for quite a few years here in Dillon. My inherent trait has been exposed. I am the culprit of such humane acts of kindness that threats of legal action have forced my choice to GO PUBLIC with my acts of compassion.

I was taught and have lived the philosophy of, "THE BEST DEEDS DONE ARE THE ONES NO ONE KNOWS ABOUT." I have no regret practicing that philosophy, especially when it comes to animals. I'm no bleeding heart or glory seeker. I have nurtured and raised many orphaned wildlife species, releasing them for a chance to live free.

We humans are responsible for domesticating dogs and cats! They too would have been "just fine" in the wild.

Our natural instinct as humans is to rule supreme over some living entity, thus the wild ancestors of our pets have evolved, submitted to training, selective breeding, and "master-minded servitude." We are the fortunate recipients of their dedication and affection.

This serves as the basis of my admission of guilt! Yes, I ensure your dog has water and a food source free of maggots and slugs! Yes, I am the culprit UNTETHERING your pet when observing they are desperate to access a dry yet empty water dish. Yes, I admit to caring for the feral cats that are abandoned when their owner moves away. Yes! I am guilty of compassion when I locate newborn kittens suffering from mutilation of cannibalism by their own "starving mother." I'm also guilty of emotional reaction when I observed 17-year-old bury a young cat up to its neck and proceed to decapitate it with a power mower. We compassionate HUMANS deplore graphic details of cruelty such as (true incident) pouring Drano crystals down a dog's throat, duct tape securing his mouth for a quieter, agonizing death. Put that scene in your head!

Omission of basic needs such as water, food, and the ability of mobility are just as cruel! Their death is merely prolonged.

Do not misconstrue my motives. I'm not on your property to take anything! I could care less what your lifestyle is. I don't CARE to know your name, so please, when you spend the time to locate my phone number to inform me of "what a blatant criminal" I am to care for your pet or chase me down in a car to state, "If you feed those cats again, I'll have you arrested," do not introduce yourself. I prefer your personal indignation at your own shortcomings (whether intentional or not) to remain ALL YOURS!

When you threaten me with calling the police and my reply is calm and unemotional as I reply, "Yes, please do," my intent is not to escalate your anger. Be advised, my attitude comes from experience. However, if this has to be a win/lose situation, I'll gladly allow you to announce your WIN, if that means a pet will be properly taken care of.

I'm so pleased to have neighbors that I consider "silent heroes." Yes, I know the fine folks who place multiple freshwater containers for the "free roamers" (dogs and cats). They, too, do so without fanfare.

I've described our summer temps as "Dante's Inferno." Imagine being in a fur coat, tethered in one small spot with either hot water to drink, or no water at all. Yes, I'm guilty! I quietly ensure your pet has adequate cool water when you are at work. I've used your own outdoor faucet to replenish your pet's water throughout the day, even providing an acceptable dish/tub for your pet. I dare say this commentary will bring more praises than insults, yet feel free to call me or chase me down to express indignation at my blatant compassion.

Joy Walsh, 805 E. Jefferson, St. Dillon . . .
Tribute to the pets "that did not make it," Summer 2004

Domino Days/Nights

If you remember the game of dominos, you know those little black rectangles displaying random white punched dots where you drew from "the bone pile," attempting to match the prominently displayed last domino. I guess the game of dominos is like playing "poker," only your cards are thicker! Well, whether you were an ace player or a novice at dominos…Doesn't it seem that the most memorable experience with these little nubs was to line them up then with all the power of a single finger and start an avalanche?

This could have been your first experience with "action and reaction." You learned quickly that strategical placement defined failure or success of your ultimate goal!

As adults, we have domino events too! Let's look at this hypothetically. After you relate to this, have a good laugh at your own domino event and never again say, "Lord, what else?" because he might just show you!

Picture this: You have an appointment with the dentist at 9:30 a.m. for a root canal. You've waited 3 weeks, suffering and losing sleep and anticipating the relief when the dentist is through.

You wake up at 11 a.m., because after walking around every night, you took a sleeping pill for one good night's sleep. You jump from your drug-induced coma to call the dentist's office. As you frantically run to the phone in the kitchen, you slam your left big toe on the door at high speed! As you continue, blinking to see through the dark shroud of pain that curtains your eyes, the cold sweat pops out. As you're dancing, wishing you could kiss instead of just cradle that wounded toe, you know that before you get to phone, not only is a cool washcloth in order, but also this allows time for your body to regain a semblance of calm. Still in that now jumpy li'l dance, you make your way down the hall to the bathroom where the cat has placed himself in the position of gate guard at the bathroom door.

Since blinded by the pain of nerve endings combined with the sweat flowing profusely into your eyes, the outcome is inevitable! And being that you don't have your glasses on, the severity has now compounded!

When you wake up in intensive care a couple days later, you question the horrible dream that transpired. The sound of a familiar, loving voice is comforting, but when you manage to open the one good eye that is not bandaged, the pained pity on your husband's face speaks pretty loudly. "Don't try to talk" is what you hear from his fuzzy image, followed by, "Darling, the surgeon assures me that your lips will be as good as new. And the wires in your jaw will only be there for 6 to 8 weeks!"

Disbelief! Well, forget facial expressions that will show your disdain. Nothing will move that should move, and all facial orifices are filled with tubes or wires. The poor appendage wounded, your big toe, is the only part of your body in sight to your one good eye. Yet, why is it suspended up so high in traction, swaddled by a cast the size of your car? *What are those rods in my leg?*

My mind, fuzzy and frenzied, attempts to take command of the hand and arm that I know is there somewhere. I see another blob of white come into my fuzzy, one-eyed world. *What . . . I think . . . forget this, I don't even wanna know!* In frustration, one can only hope there is more than one finger under that wad of hospital gauze.

With speech out of the question and every appendage "on its own," I relented to close my one good eye and drift into a drug-induced fog of oblivion. Besides, I can spend my vacation time here just as well as I could in Hawaii.

I waft out, hearing my sweet hubby saying, "Get better, baby doll. When I get back from Hawaii next week, I'll get you another kitty!"

And the positive outcome of this domino day is I no longer need that root canal since I have no teeth left!

Thus, the dominos fall!

My Close Call with the "Garden Klatch"

For the most part, I suffer "Civic Disobedience" when it comes to joining a structured organization with membership roster in excess of two members. This isn't to cast dispersion on small towns, but after 6 years of living in Dylan, South Carolina, it's obvious that the entire population has multi-memberships over and above their church!

Strangely enough, there exists the very exclusive Rio Club, established for the self-proclaimed blue bloods. Truth be known, this club exists because the entire populous does have multi-memberships! Can't be exclusive unless you build your own li'l clubhouse. This wonderful private club had no charter, creed, roll call, or charity to support. You were voted in, then played "dress up" twice a year, so I guess this Rio jokehood qualifies as "fashion police" to fellow members! Go figure!

Now, on that societal scale of uppity, the local garden clubs ranked 2nd. These units are also segregated. Membership to any one of these are obviously according to social rank. Those able to prove their lineage, those with "old money," those who "call the shots," so to speak—nothing surprising for small town society politics.

Now that the basic groundwork has been established, on with the story. Keith and I live in a quiet neighborhood, with the privilege of a wonderful park two blocks away, and since we passed it daily on our walks, the condition was monitored by "the self-appointed mayor" and assistant (yay, us!). We observed that, as play equipment was removed for repair, it never returned! As we are both impatient people, we probably failed to wait an adequate timeframe. Two years wasn't long enough! The bouncy animals left. The seesaws lost their boards, leaving perhaps "sees" but no "saw." The kiddie seat swings were rusty. The larger swings with a capacity of eight were diminished with only two remaining. Keith and I decided to be a "committee of two," discreetly completing a li'l cosmetics to add a bit more appeal. Armed with spray paints, tools (rake and shovel), and the five whimsical birdhouses Keith had constructed, we "played in our park."

It was a matter of moments before a stately little Avon-smelling woman marched toward me, haughty and offensively demanding which garden club committee I belonged to. I had to laugh when I replied, "My husband and I are self-appointed, a mutual admiration club of two." She failed to see the humor! Ms. Dinah (Keith knew her), still in a puffed-up state, inquired why we put up bird houses that had been voted as the major spring project for the rose garden club. Being the nice person I wished to be, I told Ms. Dinah that if we indeed offended her club, the birdhouses would be removed. This managed to magnify her indignance. I turned the conversation over to Keith. Now, my husband being a long-term respected "townie," I assumed he would sooth her ruffled feathers. But lo and behold! Keith commented to Ms. Dinah, "I'm the self-appointed mayor of Jefferson St., and if you object to our improvements, lodge a complaint with the city manager." My, oh my! He amazed me and agonized Ms. Dinah.

I learned that the four Garden Clubs in this fine town maintained one vegetated corner of Harmon Park. An annual pilgrimage for a newspaper photo opportunity. The question ran through my mind, "What about the rest of the year?" I thought one would need some type of yard tools to accomplish any maintenance!

For the sake of brevity, every detail of our endeavor is too numerous to write. So, in a capsule, I found out through the newspaper that I was officially the "Chairman" of Harmon Park! Also, this was the first time I knew the name of the park. So, it was there for all to see—my title imposed on the crème da la crème of Dylan society! I was gracious enough to allow a club meeting at our home (I didn't realize it would be the district members of all four clubs). Gracious ladies, yet vicious when it came to presenting potential members and voting their inclusion. Wow! This was certainly a close call with social divas at the most uppity standing. I guess you can read between the lines! You just can't be a club of two or do something because you want to! We are alright with the Iris Garden gals saving face. A labor of love needs no press—besides, if I'm unofficially official, the police will leave me alone as I wield my paint, making Dalmatians appear in the form of fire hydrants. I'm getting quite neon with the swings, and as I flip through the paper seeing the wonderful "Garden Party Luncheons" complete with Southernese attire, including straw hats, a chuckle comes from my "Spirit of Fun." I guess my invitation got lost in the mail, or perhaps my "Kindred Divas" are familiar with my hat of choice! When it comes to organizations and membership, Keith and I will remain "An Exclusive Club of Two."

Worn Out Words

It is during normal conversation with others that my brain cortex gets stuck on a word or phrase that spews into the air from someone's mouth.

On a recent visit to Luke's, he certainly halted my brain function when expressing disdain over the use of "scenario" and "awesome." He said, "They're wearing it out!" This rolled out of Luke's mouth while watching the news on TV.

Stirred within the gene pool caldron of Smiths/Whites, he was either cursed or blessed, depending on what was or is currently going on with the only male sibling present, with three sisters to perma-worry over! Though the statement was simply presented, it rings so true.

Whatever happened to the other descriptives, those adjectives that could instill the passion and understanding interjected within an otherwise intelligent commentary?

Why doesn't Stone Phillips heat up his intros on primetime by saying "groovy" or "gnarly?"

What if Barbara Walters used the likes of "super" or "kickass?"

Diane Sawyer using the term "radical" or "cool" in her segments? How about "outstanding" or "bitchin'?" Has the mutilation of such eclectic mish mush kept us from expanding our use of "in the rut" verbiage? Is there nothing that can indeed express the depth of importance of subject matters besides "awesome?"

It seems as if we need a timeframe on the use of certain slang interjected into our news, commentaries, or just everyday use of the Queen's English!

I agree with Luke—get creative, for goodness sake! Jump into Webster's or your "puter" and find "summin'" new (like I just did)! Taking it a step beyond agreement, I think Luke could come up with a dictionary with the mastery and effective use of such words as "mollygroager" and "situmahwachun," a delightful rendition borrowed from Daddy and integrated into everyday use. Good for you, Daddy! You entertained us and got your point across! I think both Paul Sr. and Jr. (aka: Luke) are Avant Garde characters—at the very least, they could never be accused of wearing it out.

Thanks for attention to this awesome scenario, Luke. You have brought awareness and humor into everyday life and listening.

Keep up the wonderful new age vocabulary! I sleep better knowing you won't "wear 'em out," and I don't care about misspelled words!

I Want One of Dem Designer Labels

Can you remember when people such as myself were referred to as eccentric, or at times a little daft. Even the term crazy was acceptable! Well, those days are gone, lost to hallowed halls of history just as religion and patriotism are stashed away to be viewed as archaic. This is in defense of our role models "of past" CARTOONS. (And you thought this was about looking through my binoculars!)

Way back, and once upon a time, television was indeed a luxury, and in black and white! It seems as though we always had a clunky TV in residence, yet it wasn't much more than a conversation piece. It honestly never mattered if it worked or not, and during "up" times, one person had to man the exterior antenna.

Our free time on Saturday mornings was spent with make-believe characters. Unlike today, we indeed knew the difference and would never attempt to re-enact stunts we viewed on the tube.

I feel the great need to dismiss any physiological or psychological labels professionals would have placed on our cartoons of old.

Consider the POPEYE characters. Wimpy would be medicated for OCD (obsessive compulsive disorder), poor Olive Oil considered Manic Depressive, Popeye himself Schizophrenic with paranoid tendencies as he mumbled to "voices in his head." And I shudder to think of the effects on those three nephews observing the bully Bluto. By the way, there is a remote chance that those three nephews were indeed the illegitimate offspring of Olive and Popeye! That's a touchy subject!

How about Mighty Mouse (my favorite)? It's absurd that a mouse can wear a cape and fly "to save the day." Well, laugh if you dare. Aren't MICKEY MOUSE and his live-in sweetie, MINNIE, the #1 profitable attraction at Disneyworld? As much as I idolized Mighty Mouse, I never understood how Oil Can Harry, the nemesis wolf to Mighty Mouse, could slither down rocks like a snake.

Remember Foghorn Leghorn, the passionate rooster? Have you noted lack of his presence? Well, in order to comply with ADA (the American Disabilities Act), Foghorn was pulled because of his stuttering. He is now attending a fully funded grant program to correct his bubonic manner of speaking (black English) and receives a tax-free federal check monthly, so he just "hangs out with the chicks." Foghorn has familiar classmates. Both Elmer Fudd and Porky Pig attend the same University receiving equal benefits.

Roadrunner symbolizes the ultimate ADHD (attention deficit hyper disorder). Thank goodness he refused medication, or I fear the coyote would fulfill his long-term obsession to torture and cannibalize the poor Roadrunner. I remind you of the sheep and cattle mutilations presently being blamed on ALIENS of the UFO kind. They are transpiring in the "backyard," so to speak, of Wiley Coyote, yet investigators dismiss the possibility of his involvement.

Poor Sylvester the Cat was refused any financial assistance from the federal programs, although he too complies with the ADA. His failure to quit "stalking" Tweety Bird has ostracized him to alley cat status, forced him to change his name to SLY and pick up bit parts in action movies, where his speech impediment serves well portraying the underdog boxer or psychotic ex-soldier.

Bugs Bunny has sadistic qualities unequalled, a combination of many psychological problems including a serious anorexic/bulimic prone eating disorder.

I can't eliminate the other "reality" shows of youth! I think social services should have investigated Uncle Sky. You know, of the SKY KING fame? He never proved his relation to that teenage "nephew" and had no visible means of support. How about MY FRIEND FLICKA? There are some serious mental maladies when the entire family holds conversation with a horse. Captain Kangaroo had a tendency to be too familiar with Dancing Bear.

Thankfully, the Saturday morning viewing for children is open and honest. Warriors, X-Men, mad bombers, Barbies (who need to buy friends), pregnant models, anorexia, bulimia, acne, extreme sports equipment (sure to get you maimed or killed), cars and trucks that are street worthy. For ages 3 and up! HOW TO instructions on DVDs, how to grow hallucinating herbs, how to build a pipe bomb, psychological games that are sure to drive Mom to madness. The list of SELF HELP for kids today is endless.

How I long to see Mighty Mouse flying across a TV screen belting out, "Here I come to save the day!"

What if My Question Doesn't Match the Keypad?

Isn't that something you wanna scream out to someone such as your phone service provider? Problem is, you can no longer get to a real human voice. What happened to these nice people we used to aggravate with such questions as, "But I know no one in Asia to call, especially for $45.00!" or "Why should I consult an attorney to interpret the coded alphabet on back of my bill?" or "If my basic service is $15.00, why does the miscellaneous charges read $76.00?"

Where did the "humans" go? If you've ever had the misfortune to attempt contact with "Ma Bell," you know the futility! That canned, computerized female voice pretending to express concern with that droll lilt factored into an irritating guide for imbeciles to answer all your mundane questions via the simple push of a keypad. Ha!

It seems as if the term "Oxymoron" applies quite fittingly when using TELEPHONE SERVICE & COMMUNICATION in the same sentence!

After sorting through the 11 pages of phone bill you receive, all by cruel design, you read the final line amount owed.

You verify that their ploy worked! The time has come! Ya gotta call and demand explanation of the redundant codes, itemized hieroglyphics, columns of what could be, and footprints of a parakeet. After all, the fine folks at the phone company are gonna amaze and dazzle you with their brilliance. RIGHT? Please! Take forewarning! All that will happen is them baffling you with bulls*** and renewing your hatred for hi-tech service.

HYPOTHETICAL THEORY: *I have a few minutes. I'll call Ma Bell before leaving for work.* In compliance with all rules listed on page 3 of your giant phonebook, you call the 20 digits listed for residential service. Success! You get the ring-a-ding that will ease all your problems! Anticipating a quick resolve, you're holding your car keys tightly, one foot out the door.

Patiently, you await the directive from the canned voice which will guide you to the proper number on the keypad to touch. Your choice of English or Spanish—#1 or #2. "Is your bill late or early?" (This question throws you off guard.) "Are you paying check or cash this current billing?" What!? "The final option…Please hold for the next available agent."

Oh, now you're back on track. You've just gotta wait a minute or so, listening to soft rock on the Muzak system they have been so kind to entertain you with. In between the subliminal advertising interjected with Muzak, there are the obvious, caring, concerned voices assuring you that "your business is important to us" and to "please continue holding" because an agent will be with you momentarily.

The picture is getting familiar. You decide to dedicate your lunch hour to resolve this. After all, there has to be a person in that office somewhere! When you decide to call "information" to obtain optional numbers, you're really gonna be surprised next billing when you see that each call you made to INFORMATION cost you $1.00! Generating additional revenue for MA BELL!

Being a civilized, professional individual, this has become a Quest, so *I'll take a day off to resolve this issue!* Get comfortable, grab a meal, and grab a copy of *War and Peace*. Once again, you get the same guide from that lovely "canned voice." After 53 repeats of "someone will be with you momentarily," the phone receiver clicks once. You hold your breath, then BEEP, BEEP, BEEP, a busy signal! By now, you are in a fetal position, whimpering, "But I followed all the directives." Forget the attempt to locate a real phone office! Somewhere out there in another dimension, there is a small metallic junction box, containing thousands of li'l fiber-optic "canned voices." They never tire, they never sleep! They have no emotion and no remorse, but they do have the ability to generate hate, discontent, and above all, a 400% inflated phone bill that we humans will pay month after month, only because it is a minor inflation when we consider time off from work to hold a receiver to our ear until it's an appendage, the cost of a prescribed anti-anxiety medication, and the cost of counseling for paranoid behavior toward all service personnel.

Oh, well. Once upon a time, we complained about the monopoly factor of phone service, the lack of choice! Guess we asked for it. As far as long-term damage caused by a receiver held to ear goes, your phone service will SELL you "head gear" just like their professionals use FOR LESS THAN A MORTGAGE! Oh, never expect "legal precedence" being spearheaded by your claim of "induced anxiety." After all, Ma Bell most likely holds major stock in pharmaceutical companies. I can't verify that claim because that question doesn't comply with the "keypad" of my touchtone phone.

FOOTNOTE: *The next time any phone service carrier calls you during your dinner hour, customize your own "vocal keypad" directive! This personally gave me an "ounce of satisfaction" to follow through with (words not printable), but if you don't feel strong enough to follow through with this, your local phone company will gladly provide a telemarketer, ZAPPER, for a nominal monthly fee.*

SPIRITUAL STORIES

Just Hold My Thought

If I happen to go away before we're together again, just hold my thought.

When you hear a laugh that reminds you of me, when you smell the aroma of fried chicken, applesauce cake, or the fragrance of my perfume, hold my thought.

When you see silly antics of an "antique little girl" willing to dance or sing with her grandchild, hold my thought.

As you pass along the "sugar bowl" to your own little girl or share the story of the angels who gently "hushed" the baby before taking wings to earth, hold my thought!

Those times in your life when the pleasure of an ice cream cone brings you a smile or times when silly sounds or antics make you laugh out loud although you aren't sure why, hold my thought!

When bright, funny colors just make you smile (like my Dr. Seuss hat) or you share a memory of fun we had, you've held my thought.

Those moments in your life when coloring or painting with another little one bring about fuzzy memories of "another time" and you smile with delight, hold my thought!

When you are a parent and grandparent, remember you thrilled me by reaching for my hand as you grabbed my heart. Emboss these simple times to your memory, then YOU HAVE HELD MY THOUGHT.

What a gift you are, so pass it on as you merely HOLD MY THOUGHT.

Written by your Onnie (heir apparent to Dr. Seuss)

I Graced Her Walk

Was it so long ago she chose me with such pride?
Fifty Years has passed since I graced this youthful bride.

My delicate lace did stand so crisp, a brilliant shade of white,
Honoring a new beginning, I hugged her waist exactly right.
I felt the beat of a heart so young; I felt the strength of love.

With her every step, my whispered serenade of satin.
With every step I graced her walk,
With every step and with every breath
I touched her anxious heart.

I served silent witness when two lives joined as one,
I served as silent witness to his promise of "forever I will love"
I served witness to the strength of his gentle hands and tender touch.
I served witness as they danced,
As they softly whispered to each other, their promise sent to God above *Fifty Years* ago.

The journey not always easy, living life takes a toll, yet here they stand together

As they promised to each other, just *Fifty Years* ago

My mantle no longer crisp and white, my satin has grown old,
the vintage lace now fragile, when once it stood so bold.
What an honor to be with her, so long we've been apart,
still, I stand as witness, still I feel her heart.

Graceful aging did so bless her, she now wears a "crown of white."
I am so blessed to be a treasure, to her I'm never old,
I offer her this special gift, "My Countenance of Pure Gold."

Written by Joy Walsh with honor and love, 2005

God's Quilt of Life

What if we received a little quilt from God when we became a true born-again Christian? Let's say about the size of a baby blanket, made of beautiful, gilded gold, silver, and translucent overlays. All that would reflect heaven.

This beautiful gift would have no directions for usage here on Earth; it would accompany us into the spiritual afterlife.

Given such a breathtaking, special icon, I think some would be tempted to place it in a vault, out of danger, out of sight. Others would most likely place it into a costly, acid-free frame displayed with honor and pride. They'd also ensure the safety with perhaps an elaborate alarm system. After all, this is a gift from GOD himself! Coveted by so many others.

I choose to use my quilt! What could be more precious than the promise of heaven wrapped around you, emitting warmth inside and out?

When I arrived before our Savior, my heavenly escort took possession of my now much larger, tattered, worn scrap! Of what was such a breathtaking gilded treasure! As I viewed the company of fellow Christians, their escorts holding forth their beautiful original treasures, I bowed my head with shame. What had I done? Surely, judgement would be harsh. The use and abuse of Heaven's treasure. I even loaned it out during my earthly ownership!

I heard the voice, so soft, ask, "Why are you ashamed to come before your father when you have such a treasure to return? I'll share with you, my child, what I see. Before me, I have someone who warmed others by loaning out your treasure. I'm pleased to see that the additions to your quilt are life experiences, both good and bad. You bring before me the tattered, frayed squares! Those I see as the adversity you suffered, wearing on your very spirit. Yes, I see the holes, the ones created by the tears you shed, those of grief, those tears of lamenting for a loved one's pain and suffering, tears of apology to me when you were less than perfect. For all the wear and tear, you did not hide your light under a bushel. You were sincere in asking forgiveness, as the mended holes reflect! For helping your fellow brothers and sisters, I thank you. Take your place in my kingdom and hold your quilt with continued love and pride. Your soul speaks through your gift back to me."

Fiction it may be, just a different slant. Who knows?

Divine Humor

Have you ever given thought to the fact that GOD has a real sense of fun? He has no problem inflicting this on or at the expense of his own creations!

This heavenly humor far exceeds the realm of understanding we miniscule humans are capable of—a fine example being a platypus. You have to admit this funny creature consists of leftovers from that 7-day marathon God made famous enough to put into print. I guess a platypus is the equivalent of the little bag of screws and stuff we always have leftover when assembling a bike or space shuttle! You get the general ideal!

I also feel like God uses the "middleman" principle about humor. He instills the knowledge within some of us humans to "pull it off." I'm not sure of his selection process; it could be a reward system or a punishment. Far be it from me to critique GOD.

If you've been fortunate enough to experience a small child expressing their view of biblical topics or saying prayers, take note that they are confused as to the exact wording voiced at meals vs. night prayers. Do you think God will send fire and brimstone if articulation and form aren't adhered to? Consider the sincerity of *"puayy lourdd bake my cake"* (*pray the Lord my soul to take*), or when a 3-year-old remembers every person, animal, and inanimate object in his/her short life by NAME while saying Grace! Talk about time standing still! How about when a child asks, "Does God have a favorite blanket?" or "Do you think God likes chocolate milk?"

I like to think the innocence of a child reaffirms that "FROM THE MOUTHS OF BABES" comes wisdom.

As long as we are blessed with children, there will be writing material. Dare to look at the universe through the eyes of a child. Dare to listen with an open heart.

Remember, we as God's children will never be corrected for sincere simplicity of prayer.

I wonder if God does like chocolate milk. Guess I'll ask!

Bleak Outlooks and Bright Lookouts

During a visit from my daughter, we had pretty much got the feather-pounding gossip out of the way, and her topic of workplace came up. Now, most would think typical whining, jealousy, or being disgruntled would rank high on her list. On the contrary. Michelle speaks highly of all of her associates, and it is obvious to me they care strongly about Michelle and my grandson, Matthew.

The complaint at hand was the mere lack of windows in the workplace, as most progressive buildings do indeed lack. This reminded me of MY dilemma many years ago concerning lack of a window in my office!

In Miami, I had a desk that looked at a wall or at the fisheye mirror I put up for entertainment. Finally, I made my own window using a box lid for depth, tissue for drawback curtains on my crayon drawing of sun, flowers, and grass. I just slapped it on my wall, and it became an icon of sorts, envied by all. Looking past the very humor of the human need to see the outside world lessening that claustrophobic sensation, my brain kickstarted into something deeper. We little miniscule humans always wish for "a rose garden in life." If we didn't suffer bleak outlooks in life, we would never appreciate true serenity when there are brighter lookouts.

Michelle, my sweet woman child! Any rose garden she knew were ones she bypassed because of thorns. I know that she is indeed "her mother's child." Each time I look in the mirror, Michelle is there. Each time she expresses indignations and lack of justice in our world, I hear myself. Obviously, the crossroad of time comes into play; I was much younger and stronger, too stubborn with my convictions! I wish time could rewind. I cheated my baby girl by not emphasizing "brighter lookouts," however I'm so pleased she and I share a deeper conviction—making our own windows for better lookouts.

I wish to give my baby girl her own "soul's window," a vista view of perpetual beauty for those times her outlooks seem bleak! I wish for her the peace of a gentle touch, that of a butterfly kiss. I wish for her to listen when discouragement sets in as she pleads for God to listen, hearing the thunder roll and the sweet sound of a bird's song, knowing he did listen.

I want her to believe in miracles—she gave birth to one! I want her to know that I admire her strength to "pick herself up, dust off, and ignore her bloody knees." I want her to always keep in mind, "When eagles dare to soar, the hunters come out."

I want my baby girl to have a reminder of harmony in blossoms, to always overcome those tears that stay on her soul, even those times pain and hurt echo through the very fiber of her life.

I want her to look through her "little" window and smile at what it represents! Most of all, I want her to know how proud I am of her, how I loved her face-cracking smiles as a baby and her contagious laughter as a woman. I need her to know that my role of Mom is not much in demand, but I sure am proud that her role to me is that of my very best friend. I love you, Michelle.

Mom

Shining For You

I now stand tall and see so clear, I shine for you, my Susie dear
You miss me so, that I know, your love has seen me through
I know your tears and all your fears, time that moves so slow
I want for you to know that the whispered breeze that blows
Is the love I send to you.

Look to the sky and you will see, a star that beams brighter and
You will know that is a kiss, especially from me
Enjoy the rain and hold no fear, for that's the showers of
Love I send to you.

I watch and wait, hoping my love can see you through
For my sweet Susie when we are joined again, our
Light will shine together forever, time that never ends.

I will be here to greet you, my sweetheart darling
And all the others too, for now you must stay behind
You have things to do.

Luke's Song

I'm tired, I'm worn, my heart is heavy from the work it takes to keep on breathing.

I've made mistakes, I've let my hope fail; my soul feels crushed by the Weight of this world.

And I know that you can give me rest, so I cry out with all that I have left

Let me see redemption win, let me know the struggle ends, that you can Mend a heart that's frail and torn.

I want to know a song can rise from the ashes of a broken life, and all that's dead Inside can be reborn.

Cause I'm worn.

I know I need to lift my eyes up, but I'm too weak. Life just won't let up and I know that you can give me rest, so I cry out with all I have left.

Let me see redemption win, let me know the struggle ends, that you can mend a heart that's frail and torn.

I want to know a song can rise from the ashes of a broken life, and all that's dead Can be reborn.

Cause I'm worn.

My prayers are wearing thin, yeah, I'm worn even before the day begins, yeah, I'm worn. I've lost the will to fight, I'm worn, so heaven come and flood my eyes.

Let me see redemption win, let me know the struggle ends, that you can mend a heart that's frail and torn. I want to know a song can rise from the ashes of a broken life, and all that's dead inside can be reborn, cause all that's dead inside, Will be reborn.

Though I'm worn, Yeah, I'm worn.

(10th Ave. North lyrics)

Heavenly Escorts

Have you ever thought of the ANGELS? I think it quite contradictive when we profess to believe in the very promise of the scripture, a supreme creator, GOD, the sacrificial lamb. Jesus' assurance of an eternal life in heaven is so beautiful, it is beyond our realm of understanding. Yet so many "Christians" are uncomfortable at the very possibility of angelic intervention here on earth.

If we as Christians have the faith to believe in the scriptures and trust in our GOD to fulfill the promise of eternal life . . . If we look in the book of Psalms 91:11, "For he shall give his angels charge over thee, to keep thee in all thy ways" or in the book of Hebrew 13:2, "Be not forgetful to entertain strangers for thereby some have entertained ANGELS UNAWARE." I surely have no intention of convincing anyone to believe my own experiences with what I have no doubt was angelic intervention! I do share the different experiences. Let others judge as to whether ole Joy needs an anti-psychotic drug regime or if my faith rings truth.

First, I don't believe that we human beings become these "winged, translucent, glorious figures" we see depicted as angels. Angels, just as humans, were created by the divine with the purpose of protecting and guiding. They even battle evil on Earth. I also believe there is a chain of command within the ranks of angelic beings, and also the capability to assume any form conducive for their given task. Why don't we see them? How do you know you haven't encountered one or more angelic interventions in your lifetime?

This isn't a new age thought process I have acquired, and if anyone had tried to tell me even six years ago that there were angels here on Earth, I would have referred them to a psychiatric care program! However, with my "homecoming" to my faith, a new babe in my religious belief, my heart was softened. If confession is good for the soul, I guess this is a valid confession that I don't feel like I was a very good person! I watched Mama on her knees at night, deep in prayer, and this always made me squeamish. I know she had strong faith, and I feel like Daddy obtained peace before his passing. Through adversity in a "plastic, mannequin lifestyle," there was no peace, no security, no safe haven, nothing positive for me to pass onto the ones I loved the most. Thus, my hardness became their burden to engrain on their soul. I sent my children to church sometimes but did not take them! I see the turmoil in their adulthood and grieve for the role I played.

I pray for our Lord's intervention, to send his angels to shield and protect Brad, Michelle, Matthew, Elizabeth, and Jessica in their jobs, school, everyday living, and decision making. It seems that when I send out one of those soft-whispered prayers, the tiniest ones from your heart, the results are made apparent!

I too believe there are times when we are truly tested. Have you ever had the opportunity to encounter or be encountered by an individual seemingly not a "desirable," yet feel compelled to take an action you normally would not do? Let's take for example a trip to Walmart, a quick in and out trip. But when the hand of a squatty, toothless senior citizen touches your arm requesting help with finding batteries, although you are rushed, somehow this task becomes "yours"—not an employee's. A timeframe of 15-20 minutes is spent, and as you hand her each package to analyze, you feel patience.

Let me tell you about how peaceful and calm her presence made me feel! Let me tell you how, in seconds, she was nowhere to be found. Although her steps were slow and deliberate, let me tell you how a far off "thank you" was whispered behind my head as I searched the aisles. Let me tell you about the serenity that stayed with me all evening. Many times,

I thought of the alternatives to this situation, and the "angels unaware" always came to the forefront.

I also know that angelic intervention that is meant for you can and has been witnessed by other everyday people, yet you see nothing!

On the third Wednesday of November 1999, I had been working in and out of the house, never locking storm doors, never feeling a threat in my neighborhood. For the most part, I was the only person home all day.

The Lockemy Residence across the street had several service personnel installing a new heat pump system, so they were going about their business, as I was. I was startled when I walked through the hall toward a propped-open front storm door (propped open so cats could come and go), and there were two young men—one on the top step, the other right behind him on sidewalk with his eyes scanning. It's one of those times the hair stands up on your neck and your pulse quickens! I immediately remembered a dream similar to this situation where the outcome wasn't good.

The man on my step mumbled something inaudible. I think it was about a magazine or paper. They had nothing in their hands that led me to think solicitation. The young man on the sidewalk kept his eyes scanning, slapped his friend on the shoulder, and they both bolted across my front yard across Jefferson St. They continued running down 14th St. until they were out of sight. I was relieved and dismissed the incident, closing and locking the front door.

Later in the morning, one of the guys hollered across the street to me (most of these gentlemen knew Keith). I walked across street, and he asked, "Where's that work crew from? The guys I saw earlier when you were so busy?" Thinking in real time, I flippantly said something about the two young men who were questionable and that I should keep my doors closed. Another worker came around from the back of the house (Lockemy), and he said, "I know one of them boys. He's bad news! Good thing you had your own football team there with you."

I was walking back across the street, stopped, walked back to the worker and the supervisor, and asked, "What are you talking about?" I was being as casual about the question as I could tactfully be. After all, NO ONE was in my yard! It was a thought process that did not register with me. After all, they were sane, responsible men, obviously making conversation in an honest, inquisitive nature as to "my own burly, dress-in-whites work crew." They asked where they were contracted from, since none of the guys had seen them come to our house via vehicle, nor had they noticed them leave! I mumbled something, walked to the house, sat down on edge of the front porch, and tried to put logic to what I DID NOT SEE. When Keith came in for lunch, I think I was still sitting there. I repeated what had happened.

ANGELS UNAWARE? My question was, why didn't I witness their presence? It was obvious intervention on my behalf. After all this time, I think it was to validate the very presence of angels. After all, when an entire crew of workers across the street saw them, how do I question that? The way the entire broken conversation went was that of "small town chat," curious as to the identity of just another group of workers. Even when in a jovial, entertained manner, one of the guys commented on the two guys that "rabbited" off of my property, hightailing it past the two illusive figures who were leaning on our mailbox. These "burly men in white" stationed all over our yard were reality to others—just not to me.

I thought about discussing this in detail with these "real" people, but Keith and I discussed it and decided against it. After all, I would appear to be the blind one! There was no doubt that there was a presence in our yard that day in November, and no doubt that the two who ran away did so in fright!

You decide! I'll take any logical explanation. There was no feeling of "divine intervention," no great spiritual cleansing feeling—just puzzled and still sweating from my own real yard work! It was indeed a memorable event.

How about another time, visiting Michelle and Matthew in Shallotte, North Carolina in the spring of 2001? Keith and I were taking her a patio set. I was feeling a bit overwhelmed by the plight she was in emotionally and physically. Keith and I had made some small talk over it while watching Matthew enjoy playing in the truck. I mentioned to Keith, "All I can do is pray for the angels to watch over and be with them."

The good thing about having a digital camera is the fact it is almost impossible to have "light bleed in," and the quality has always been outstanding. So, without getting into detail or being wordy, see the picture. You decide! Although Matthew is a blonde, this kind of blinding light isn't a reflection or light bleeding in! You decide... I truly believe my prayers were acknowledged.

If we have the promise of the scripture, then the angels are here for us. Some may say that little voice is your conscience. Perhaps that's true; Lord knows I've heard my conscience over the years. But I think that, living 50 years, I know the difference between the two.

Finally, before you judge me as a "wacko" or fanatic, speak to anyone associated with Hospice, or in some cases, EMTs or police officers. If comfortable with the situation, any one of these can affirm that when you're in the midst of a person dying, there is definitely a strange feeling that comes over those present! The general common thread that each have stated is the shaky, trembling, pressing feeling—a breathless, time-standing, still air in the room.

One police officer spoke to me with the emotional tone and conviction of, "I felt his soul pass through me!" This was as he cradled a dying victim of a traffic accident. How can you dismiss this? This officer described the trembling of his entire body and the pressing feeling of "presences unseen" around him on that street.

Father, Do I Have to Go?

Yes, I hear you and have heard you for some time. Guess I'm selfish for wanting to stay. You have been so generous and patient . . .

You have walked a path so many of my children do, those times you felt so alone in the wilderness of dark despair, to leave with no hope, broken spirited, and a lost soul! You needed extra time to find your way back home.

Will they be okay if I leave with no goodbye? Are there enough good memories to ease the shame I feel at the bad ones?

Do you think you're my only child to feel that way? None of you are perfect—just human! They will be okay.

You always spoke of that "longest walk," and remember how much you recall the good lessons your Mama instilled? The humble, simple phrases of your Daddy? Does that ease your concern?

I could make more excuses. That's human too! Such as, "Got more stuff to do," or "I'm not ready," but in truth, I'm so very scared and not sure what to do. You know every secret, every mean, unkind thought and act I'm so guilty of. Even now, scraps of being contrite hang around, words that aren't so nice, and I really, really try to be the child you created me to be.

Do you truly have faith? I KNOW your fear. Did you think I forgot you because you blamed me for so long? Think I stopped loving you when you cursed the very heavens only because you felt so abandoned by others and weakened? You forgot the promise, "I will never forsake you." That battle with darkness isn't new to me, yet I don't always win!

I've lost many children as evil whispers, sweetly and convincingly. My children are precious, and the loss of just one is enough to make all Heaven cry and mourn, so can you understand to save one as you make way for celebration in Heaven?

There are no words to describe your eternal mansion. When you join the chorus, you will understand. How can I help you? Ask what questions you feel will ease your trip; despair is not the baggage you should bring along.

I'm so ashamed, Father, for those times I hated you so, even as the words and thoughts blamed you for "allowing" these bad things. You KNOW I really hated me for my "independent, self-serving attitude!" Those temptations we humans experience come in pretty and enticing packages, and the evil that whispers sweet words of encouragement to be and act independent of you, my Father, can truly steal the gift of "free will" you blessed me with.

Joy, "I will never and have never forsaken you." My love is unconditional!

Would You Know a Broken Soul?

WOULD YOU KNOW A BROKEN SOUL, a daily voice and face in life? Would you know such lifeless eyes, or did you look away so as not to see the pain and strife?

Have you ever heard the silent cries, or touched a grieving heart? The desperate need for your love so long has been ignored. Is there so very much that love can't heal with its strong and magical touch?

WOULD YOU KNOW AN EMPTY HEART, so full of fear and guilt, to bear the pain takes a special strength, a strength no longer there?

WOULD YOU KNOW A BROKEN SOUL, or a heart that has no place? The love you chose to turn away breaks the soul and swirls in the mind like a bitter cold wind on the heart and face.

WOULD YOU KNOW A BROKEN SOUL, a heart rejected, one never to share your dreams and goals? A broken soul that kicked and screamed for your comfort or such words as, "It's okay . . . I love you and understand."

Your words, "I've never loved you, so make a brand-new start," takes more than you desire and simply can 't be done with an empty, broken heart.

You kept your love for all these years, to show and share with others. The grief that floods my heart still keeps a love for you that could never be for another. Take that, too—it has no place with an empty, broken soul.

The tears on a face can be swiftly swept away. The tears that fall on a broken soul will forever with me stay.

PATRIOTIC STORIES

Patriots Still Serving

The anniversary of the day that "Will Live in Infamy" approaches. There aren't words describing the dark days of Pearl Harbor, but for my generation and those yet to be born, it is a bleak, stark reality and devastating history in the making.

I am reflecting back to ascertain the exact depth of emotion, the degree of shock and disbelief, wanting so desperately to make this go away! We joined as a nation to rally support for those we could not physically offer a shoulder or caring hand to. We found it necessary to reach deep into our very souls to stand tall for each other, to stand even taller for the children, protecting their fragile world. Reassuring them, reaffirming security in their limited realm of understanding.

Within hours, the "Symbol of Freedom," our American flag, the red, white, and blue, became a reinforced symbol of our unity, the common threads of freedom and tenacious spirit. Sadly, we have all been guilty of "shelving" this beautiful flag, bringing it out on Independence Day, Memorial and Flag Day—if we remember to do so.

As I look back on the total surreal landscape of New York City after the attack, the Pentagon, the very heart of our defense program, the lonely, dark, gaping hole in Pennsylvania...The first reaction was to fly our flag, our symbol of unity, the American spirit.

It is difficult to express the awe of the beautiful American flag waving from the top of the towers of New York, a silent sentry, not just surviving but was retrieved to carry on, duty bound. Watching the Olympics opening ceremony where the somber presentation of the scarred, tattered icon of our freedom was carried out before the mass crowd. The grief of loss overwhelmed me and the amazement that a mere manmade fabric, woven into this beautiful symbol, could indeed survive when everything and everyone below this billowing beauty did not!

The scenes of total carnage, inhumanity, death, and grief was a true test of strength and faith. As we cried out, lamenting the loss, we looked to our symbol of unity and strength.

The gnarled, tangled, overwhelming mountain of steel, concrete, and glass became a view to hell, an abyss of unending horrors, sounds, smells, and wails of grief. We anxiously watched as disappointment came in waves. Yet a silent sentinel lay below and was quietly retrieved—a small miracle. Yes, the flag had survived.

With deeper respect to the "red, white, and blue" and sacrifices made for this proud symbol, I received comfort from a new observation as to the "spirit" of America and Americans, both present and past.

All of Manhattan, blinded by the smoke, dust, sounds, and smells, was brought to its very knees, the congested hub of our financial center stripped and feeling very alone and small. As I watched the busy motion of those involved, hundreds of men and women, I noticed they had the same stare of hollow disbelief, working totally on adrenalin and the movement of autopilot.

Looking around, the devastation seemed to stretch for miles, each scene reflecting the horror of reality. And in the dusky, smokey stench, a twinkling of an incredible event—the beautiful American flag was retrieved. How could this be?

I switched gears in my imagination, seeing much more than the reality of what was transpiring. As the flag was being reverently brought into the light, the unseen hands of our past patriots were also present. Still diligent to duty, I see the likes of Henry "Hap" Arnold, ensuring the grommet at the top of our stars wasn't entangled on jagged edges, followed by the likes of Creighton Abrams holding his corner with the same tenderness used to cradle dying troops in an Asian jungle. Stephen Decatur was rising into view, his vintage uniform as sharp as the day he put it on and took oath.

Such military men of distinction, assisting the living to ensure our beautiful flag was freed to serve again! Looking with dropped jaw at such a scene. It wasn't surprising to see figures wafting from that crevice. Those dusting their hands and uniforms, displaying a misty look of intensity. Somehow, I knew these men.

The 19-year-old corporal who lost his life in the jungle of Vietnam when he stood his ground in order to save others, the tattered appearance of a hollow face, covered in shreds of what was the proud uniform of the 101st Airborne, this "Screaming Eagle" sacrifice on that long journey near the 38th parallel, unassuming, gangly. He was no leader of notoriety—just a husband and father of a son (a patriot, not surprisingly). The figure of an airman, gnarled legs, festering wounds, rags of his uniform still apparent, perched atop a heap of smoky metal, as proud of his duty to flag and country as he was when he slipped out of his life at the Hanoi Hilton. These are the phantoms of the past who, in another act of unselfish obligation to their country, threw themselves upon that beloved flag as it tumbled underneath the rubble.

I was amazed, yet not surprised, when taking in a larger scope of this scene. The busy workers were observed and encouraged by hundreds of these "spirits" who had ultimately died for the honor of freedom—invisible color guards of our "red, white, and blue." Reality of the price paid for the honor of displaying "old glory" deepened.

Standing staunch and proud, visions of history punched through the fabric of time, with Omar Bradley and George Patton seemingly taking command of the objective. Douglas McArthur was to their immediate left, complete with unlit pipe squeezed between lips, observing the scene with proud, unwavering eyes.

When others would be silent as they passed bucket after bucket, hoping to retrieve some closure to a "life lost," there was a chorus of pride being emitted from these phantom soldiers. What I would perceive as "deafening" to the masses was disregarded, yet somehow the knowledge of such renewed spirit was indeed a physical rekindling of those rejoicing at the retrieval of such a fragile icon, the American flag.

These were the heroes of past, inundating the scenes of destruction. Perhaps whispering to us all, we knew what our fate was, yet we ran to greet it. The indelible spirit of what inspired these to lose their lives for the freedom of their country and the liberties we have taken for granted.

Chester Nimitz was surveying the waterways leading into the New York docks, ready to assist with the protection of our coastal waters. He wore the same bulldog poker face that was a major wedge to those enemies in the Pacific. Alongside him in silent repose stood Walter Krueger—an awesome duo, hellbent on a mission of continued liberty and freedom for the people of America.

Absorbed in the very numbers of past leaders and unsung heroes, it was comforting to see Philip Sheridan and Jubel Early mustering their troops into a single unit—enemies during a time of rift in young America, but brothers in arms at a time tinsel strength was needed. And as the blue and gray mist of uniforms meshed, so did the stars and bars, and the stars and stripes—unity for their America.

So, understanding was at last realized. That tattered flag of old glory survived with the assistance of those souls who did not hesitate to die for their country, securing freedom for future generations and following their symbol into battle, motivated and proud to serve.

I feel that we can all take comfort that these "heroes of the past" live on, proud of their flag, proud of generations that followed them, always at the ready to encourage the weary and reinforce our symbols of freedom, respecting the ultimate price they were willing to pay.

It is with resolve that I ponder those who have joined these heroes of the past—the average citizen, men and women willing to sacrifice their life for us all. So, if you are in the area of a Pennsylvania meadow, the seat of our democracy, Washington, D.C., or taking in a show on Broadway, you too may glance up, or at the corner of your eye see a fleeting image of a crusty WWII hero. Whether you're walking with a businessman or airline stewardess, even the image of a group of friends obviously of our century, mingled with those of another time, patronizing the Tomb of the Unknown Soldier.

The ranks have increased in number. The ones to render their all for our beautiful flag of freedom fly it proudly. When saying the Pledge of Allegiance, ask yourself, "Do I know the depth of that pledge?" Would you give your life for an allegiance to God and to your country? Something to think about.

* *Additional dedication to Michael Scott Speicher (1-13-05), a patriot friend giving closure to some personal agonies. Scotty is indeed the "Patriot's Saint."*

Epilogue

I'm assuming that if you, the reader, have reached this page, then at least you've flipped through my labor of love! My esoteric style of writing is not for everyone and isn't meant to be!

It would be so sad if our great grandchildren failed to remember that Ed Bowers was an extraordinary carver or that Mary Ellen was the classiest lady one could ever imagine! Or that Patty had qualities she herself never acknowledged. Who would care that she painted an entire house BY HERSELF at 16? Yes, I remember! Or that Luke has suffered more heartbreak than all of us combined? That Barb bought me my topaz jewelry? That Jim took us all in his green Ford to get our shots? That Bill was ostracized and did okay in spite of it? I also remember Minnie's trip to Washington, D.C when she was a teen. I remember Luke's car, FROGGY! I remember Patty falling down an entire flight of steps with scalding water. I remember feeling responsible. I remember Barb's red and white Ford (and the windows knocked out of it). I remember the night Minnie got her engagement ring. I remember the first time Luke was introduced to Brit after his return from Vietnam. I remember sleigh rides down Columbia Ave. I remember raisin pie aroma when Barb baked. I remember the mysterious, strange uniforms worn by J. Pyatte, Jim, and Bill. I remember it was no mystery when Luke wore a similar uniform into battle. I remember boiling grasshoppers, playing pinball in the old Columbia Ave. barn, picking wild violets and wild strawberries.

Thanks to Minnie sharing her time, I remember Daddy crying with me after losing Buster. I remember Mama crying when she lost her Daddy. I remember my wooden, handmade, green wheelbarrow, my handmade highchair, my tears and wounds wiped away the time I almost fell off Fairview Ave. Bridge. I remember mustard and onion sandwiches with red Kool-Aid. I remember the innocence of two sisters (Patty and I) attempting to create another kid just by soaking a baby picture in water overnight! I remember the loss of a baby rabbit I so desperately wanted to save.

I could speak volumes with these simple memories, but I just can't be selective! So, I accept the fact that what I try to share in the "little things," I certainly am thankful that the photos of the smokehouse, highchair, nature prints, and such do exist. Someday, those very tangible icons of our existence will be shrugged off as "never was, never happened," and so the fiction writing continues.

This epilogue isn't open for group discussion. Private use is prohibited due to mental status being misunderstood. After all, what you are reading is imaginary, so just forget it.

PRESENTED IN THE SPIRIT OF EXACTLY HOW IT IS STATED.

I love you all! Thanks for the memories, real or created.